PROSE: AN ANTHOLOGY

FOR KEY STAGE 4

IMELDA PILGRIM

Nelson Thornes

Published in 2013 by:
Nelson Thornes Ltd
Delta Place
27 Bath Road
CHELTENHAM
GL53 7TH
United Kingdom

13 14 15 16 17 / 10 9 8 7 6 5 4 3 2 1

A catalogue record for this book is available from the British Library

ISBN 978 1 4085 2194 6

Illustrations by Bridget Dowty, Andrew Elkerton and Paul McCaffrey

Page make-up by Pantek Media, Maidstone, Kent

Printed and bound in Spain by GraphyCems

Contents

Section A
Fiction

1 I Used to Live Here Once – Jean Rhys   5
2 We Were Just Driving Around – Jon McGregor   7
3 The Baddies – Charles Dickens   9
4 Something Wicked This Way Comes – Ray Bradbury   10
5 Small Island – Andrea Levy   14
6 The Secret of Crickley Hall – James Herbert   16
7 The Invisible Man – H. G. Wells   18
8 On the Sidewalk Bleeding – Evan Hunter   22
9 The Photograph – Sefi Atta   26
10 A Sunrise on the Veldt – Doris Lessing   28
11 The Evening Gift – R. K. Narayan   30

Section B
Literary Non-Fiction

1 The Beggar King – Aminatta Forna   36
2 Work Your Way Around The World – Susan Griffith   38
3 Fall of Antwerp, October 1914 – Sergeant Richard Tobin   40
4 Tickling the English – Dara O Briain   42
5 I Have Lived A Thousand Years – Livia Bitton-Jackson   45
6 Samuel Pepys: The Unequalled Self – Claire Tomalin   49
7 The Sunday Morning Markets – Henry Mayhew   52
8 Taking a Picture – Vivienne de Watteville   54
9 Getups – Maya Angelou   56
10 My Father's Fortune – Michael Frayn   58
11 The New Boy – Dirk Bogarde   59
12 Mawson's Will – Lennard Bickel   63

Section C
Journalism

1 Keep the flame alive: the Olympic legacy and the new country we could be – *Daily Telegraph*   67
2 Give a life-changing gift this Christmas – *The Guardian*   70
3 A letter to… my 14 year-old daughter – *The Guardian*   72
4 Disaster – *The Daily Mirror*   74
5 A tragedy remembered: Aberfan, the village that lives in the shadow of the past – *The Independent*   75
6 Hurray for teenagers – *The Guardian*   78
7 One perfect hour with Uganda's mountain gorillas – *Wanderlust*   82
8 3.56am: man steps on the moon – *The Guardian*   84
9 How technology is taking hold of our children's lives – *The Telegraph*   86
10 Skyfall Reviews   88
11 Japan earthquake and tsunami: 'we had no idea how much worse it would get' – *The Guardian*   91
12 Photographs of the Japan earthquake and tsunami damage   94
13 Don McCullin: celebrated war photographer on the value of his craft – *The Huffington Post UK*   95

Fiction

What is fiction?

It is easy to say that fiction is made up: a work of the imagination. In many ways this is true. Stories about vampires, aliens and deep-sea monsters start in the imagination of their writers, as do stories about schools, detectives, adventures and extraordinary events. However, those same writers also draw on what they know to create their works of fiction. The worlds they create and the characters who inhabit these worlds must be convincing so that the readers can identify with them and, for the time of reading, believe in them.

New Worlds

At its best, fiction not only opens up new worlds to us, but also makes us look again at the world in which we live. It challenges us to think hard about a range of complex issues. It prompts us to reflect on our own personal relationships. It raises our awareness of other cultures and other ways of thinking, and informs our knowledge of historical and current events. Most of all, it engages and absorbs us with the power of its story.

There are millions of stories written over time and across the world. What makes the best stand out is the way they are told. A good story can fail badly in the hands of a poor writer. The best writers craft their stories skilfully, choosing words to paint pictures of people, places and events, and to engage the minds and emotions of their readers.

New Experiences

How we respond to a work of fiction will depend, in part, on our own experiences and personalities. Some people love horror stories, some love mystery and others love those set in historical times. But, whatever our current favourites, we should aim to remain open to new experiences and new worlds.

The 11 short stories and extracts from longer works of fiction in this section have been chosen because we hope you will find something to interest you and to learn from in each of them. They cover a range of subject matters and demonstrate a range of writing skills, some of which you may want to introduce into your own writing. They are, however, just a starting point from which you can further explore the wonderful world of fiction.

Source 1 | I Used to Live Here Once

This short story is set in the writer's homeland of Dominica in the Caribbean. A woman returns to a place she once knew well but all is not as it once was…

She was standing by the river looking at the stepping stones and remembering each one. There was the round unsteady stone, the pointed one, the flat one in the middle – the safe stone where you could stand and look around. The next wasn't so safe for when the river was full the water flowed over it and even when it showed dry it was slippery. But after that it was easy and soon she was standing on the other side.

The road was much wider than it used to be but the work had been done carelessly. The felled trees had not been cleared
10 away and the bushes looked trampled. Yet it was the same road and she walked along feeling extraordinarily happy.

It was a fine day, a blue day. The only thing was that the sky had a glassy look that she didn't remember. That was the only word she could think of. Glassy. She turned the corner, saw that what had been the old pave had been taken up, and there too the road was much wider, but it had the same unfinished look.

She came to the worn stone steps that led up to the house and her heart began to beat. The screw pine was gone, so
20 was the mock summer house called the ajoupa, but the clove tree was still there and at the top of the steps the rough lawn stretched away, just as she remembered it. She stopped and looked towards the house that had been added to and painted white. It was strange to see a car standing in front of it.

There were two children under the big mango tree, a boy and a little girl, and she waved to them and called 'Hello', but they didn't answer her or turn their heads. Very fair children, as Europeans born in the West Indies so often are: as if the white blood is asserting itself against all the odds.

30 The grass was yellow in the hot sunlight as she walked towards them. When she was quite close, she called again, shyly: 'Hello'. Then, 'I used to live here once,' she said. Still they didn't answer. When she had said for the third time 'Hello' she was quite near them.

Her arms went out instinctively with the longing to touch them. It was the boy who turned. His gray eyes looked straight into hers. His expression didn't change. He said, 'Hasn't it gone cold all of a sudden. D'you notice? Let's go in.' 'Yes, let's,' said the girl. Her arms fell to her sides as she watched them running across the grass to the house. That was the first time

40 she knew.

by Jean Rhys

**Source 2 |
We Were Just
Driving Around**

A young man recalls
in detail the events
of a car journey with
friends, showing
how an ordinary,
everyday event can
suddenly become
a newspaper
headline.

We were just driving around.

It was late in the evening but it was still light. We'd been out for hours and it was one of those nights when it seemed like basically it was never going to get dark. We hadn't seen anyone around, and a couple of times when we'd stopped and got out it had been totally quiet, like normal, but we had the music turned up loud in the car and it made things seem sort of hectic or like picturesque? With how far you could see across the fields, and the speed, and the light, and the music?
10 Like when you're walking around with headphones on and it makes everything seem like a film? Like that. Anyway.

Josh was talking about setting up a business selling handmade snacks. He said he wasn't going to go to university, he was going to make his fortune straight out of school. His big idea was that you could get these like gourmet snacks made to order, right there in the shop. It would be like the deli-counter of the munchie world, he was saying. He was laughing about it, but he was totally serious, he was laughing because he thought it was so brilliant. Any flavour you want, he was
20 saying, any snack you want! I'll be a millionaire! He sounded like someone off *The Apprentice*. He was listing all the snacks he could think of, crisps and pretzels and Bombay mix and popcorn, and what they were all made of, and he was talking about how the economics of it were brilliant. Pennies into pounds, my friends! He kept shouting that. Pennies into pounds! He was shouting because the music was so loud but also because he was so excited about it? I didn't really get it. Anyway.

Tom wanted to know if this shop was going to be located round here and if so then where did Josh think his customer
30 base was going to come from? It didn't look like Josh had thought about that. He waved his hand around a bit, meaning: like, around here somewhere? I don't know yet, he said. There's people around though, there's like a widely distributed customer base, yeah? He pointed to a farmhouse over on the right, three or four fields away, and then another one a bit further off, the other side of the river. The lights in the windows were just coming on so it must have been a bit darker by then than it seemed. There you go, he said, that's two of them right there. Tom said, what, are you going to do it
40 like mobile? A mobile crisp van? Josh leaned over and punched

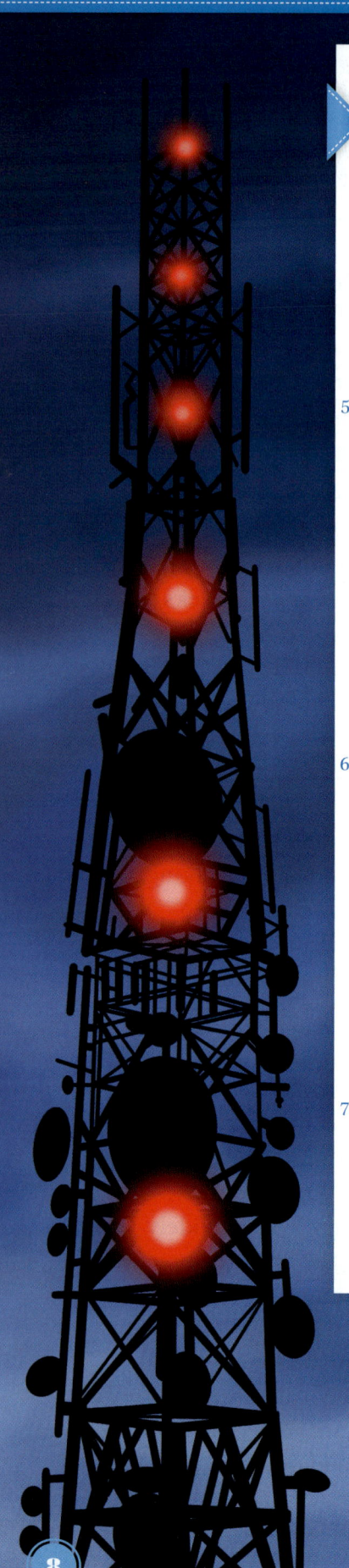

him in the shoulder, and it was sort of a play-punch but he sort of meant it as well. No one said anything for a minute. It was just the music and the sound of the tyres on the road. I wasn't even sure where we were. I could see the red lights of some television mast or something, and the sky all shadowy blue behind it. We went over a little bridge and it felt like the tyres left the road for a second. I don't think Josh even knew where we were going. Josh said, don't take the piss mate. This is serious, this is totally serious. This is going to work, yeah?
50 It's like, a totally unfulfilled market niche. And I'll be filling in that niche, big-time.

That got us laughing for a bit, about Josh filling in an unfulfilled niche.

Tom wouldn't let it go though, he was giving it all the economic model and the population density and the vulnerability of depending on impulse purchases and Josh was all nodding but then he goes Tom mate you don't get it. You don't get it. I'm talking about handmade gourmet snack products. Made to order! Like locally sourced! They'll come
60 pouring in from every direction! They'll be queuing up outside! He cut the music and put on this solemn face and a deep voice like from a film trailer and goes: If you fry it, they will come.

That set us all laughing again. The state we were in, it didn't take much? Plus Josh had this very high-pitched laugh that was pretty infectious, and once he'd got us all going it was just about impossible to stop? It just kept sort of growing, getting louder and louder, like something sort of swelling up until it filled the car and we couldn't hardly breathe and the noise of it was making me dizzy and then Amanda said Josh will you slow
70 down a bit and he turned round to ask her what she'd said so that must have been how come he never saw the corner?

by Jon McGregor

Source 3 | The Baddies

The 19th century writer Charles Dickens created some bizarre and wonderful characters. Some of these were very good and some were downright evil! These extracts introduce the reader to two such 'baddies'.

The child was closely followed by an elderly man of remarkably hard features and forbidding aspect, and so low in stature as to be quite a dwarf, though his head and face were large enough for the body of a giant. His black eyes were restless, sly, and cunning; his mouth and chin, bristly with the stubble of a coarse hard beard; and his complexion was one of that kind which never looks clean or wholesome. But what added most to the grotesque expression of his face was a ghastly smile, which, appearing to be the mere result of habit and to have no connection with any mirthful or complacent feeling, constantly revealed the few discoloured fangs that were yet scattered in his mouth, and gave him the aspect of a panting dog. His dress consisted
10 of a large high-crowned hat, a worn dark suit, a pair of capacious shoes, and a dirty white neckerchief sufficiently limp and crumpled to disclose the greater portion of his wiry throat. Such hair as he had was of a grizzled black, cut short and straight upon his temples, and hanging in a frowzy fringe about his ears. His hands, which were of a rough, coarse grain, were very dirty; his fingernails were crooked, long, and yellow.

Quilp in *The Old Curiosity Shop*

"Come in, you sneaking warmint; wot are you stopping outside for, as if you was ashamed of your master! Come in!"

The man who growled out these words, was a stoutly-built fellow of about five-and-thirty, in a black velveteen coat, very soiled drab breeches, lace-up half boots, and grey cotton stockings, which inclosed a bulky pair of legs, with large swelling calves;- the kind of legs, which in such costume, always look in an unfinished and incomplete state without a set of fetters to garnish them. He had a brown hat on his head, and a dirty belcher handkerchief round his neck: with the long frayed ends of which he smeared the beer from his face as he spoke. He disclosed, when he had done so, a broad heavy
10 countenance with a beard of three days' growth, and two scowling eyes; one of which displayed various parti-coloured symptoms of having been recently damaged by a blow.

"Come in, d'ye hear?" growled this engaging ruffian.

A white shaggy dog, with his face scratched and torn in twenty different places, skulked into the room.

Bill Sykes in *Oliver Twist*

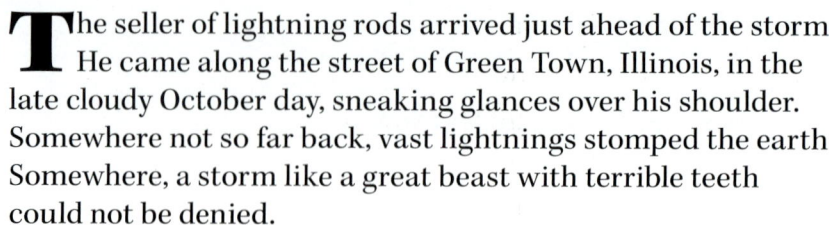

The seller of lightning rods arrived just ahead of the storm. He came along the street of Green Town, Illinois, in the late cloudy October day, sneaking glances over his shoulder. Somewhere not so far back, vast lightnings stomped the earth. Somewhere, a storm like a great beast with terrible teeth could not be denied.

So the salesman jangled and clanged his huge leather kit in which oversized puzzles of ironmongery lay unseen but which his tongue conjured from door to door until he came at last to
10 a lawn which was cut all wrong.

No, not the grass. The salesman lifted his gaze. But two boys, far up the gentle slope, lying *on* the grass. Of a like size and general shape, the boys sat carving twig whistles, talking of olden or future times, content with having left their fingerprints on every movable object in Green Town during summer past and their footprints on every open path between here and the lake and there and the river since school began.

'Howdy, boys!' called the man all dress in storm-colored clothes. 'Folks home?'

20 The boys shook their heads.

'Got any money, yourselves?'

The boys shook their heads.

'Well—' The salesman walked about three feet, stopped and hunched his shoulders. Suddenly he seemed aware of house windows or the cold sky staring at his neck. He turned slowly, sniffing the air. Wind rattled the empty trees. Sunlight, breaking through a small rift in the clouds, minted a last few oak leaves all gold. But the sun vanished, the coins were spent, the air blew gray; the salesman shook himself from his spell.

30 The salesman edged slowly up the lawn.

'Boy,' he said. 'What's your name?'

And the first boy, with hair as blond-white as milk thistle, shut up one eye, tilted his head, and looked at the salesman with a single eye as open, bright and clear as a drop of summer rain.

'Will,' he said. 'William Halloway.'

The storm gentleman turned. 'And *you*?'

The second boy did not move, but lay stomach down on the autumn grass, debating as if he might make up a name. His hair
40 was wild, thick, and the glossy color of waxed chestnuts. His eyes, fixed to some distant point within himself, were mint rock-crystal green. At last he put a blade of dry grass in his casual mouth.

'Jim Nightshade,' he said.

The storm salesman nodded as if he had known it all along.

'Nightshade. That's quite a name.'

'And only fitting,' said Will Halloway. 'I was born one minute *before* midnight, October thirtieth. Jim was born one minute *after* midnight, which makes it October thirty-first.'

'Halloween,' said Jim.

50 By their voices, the boys had told the tale all their lives, proud of their mothers, living house next to house, running for the hospital together, bringing sons into the world seconds apart; one light, one dark. There was a history of mutual celebration behind them, Each year Will lit the candles on a single cake at one minute to midnight. Jim, at one minute after, with the last day of the month begun, blew them out.

So much Will said, excitedly. So much Jim agreed to, silently. So much the salesman, running before the storm, but poised here uncertainly, heard looking from face to face.

'Halloway. Nightshade. No money, you say?'

The man, grieved by his own conscientiousness, rummaged in his leathery bag and seized forth an iron contraption.

'Take this, free! Why? One of those houses will be struck by lightning! Without this 60 rod, Bang! Fire and ash, roast pork and cinders! Grab!'

The salesman released the rod. Jim did not move. But Will caught the iron and gasped.

'Boy, it's heavy! And funny-looking. Never seen a lightning rod like this. Look, Jim!'

And Jim, at last, stretched like a cat, and turned his head. His green eyes got big and then very narrow.

The metal thing was hammered and shaped half-crescent, half-cross. Around the rim of the main rod little curlicues and doohingies had been soldered on later. The entire surface of the rod was finely scratched and etched with strange languages, names that could tie the tongue or break the jaw, numerals that added to incomprehensible sums, pictographs of insect-animals all bristle, chaff and claw.

70 'That's Egyptian.' Jim pointed his nose at a bug soldered to the iron. 'Scarab beetle.'

'So it is, boy!'

Jim squinted. 'And those there—Phoenician hen tracks.'

'Right!'

'Why?' asked Jim.

'Why?' said the man. 'Why the Egyptian, Arabic, Abyssinian, Choctaw? Well, what tongue does the wind talk? What nationality is a storm? What country do rains come from? What color is lightning? Where does thunder go when it dies? Boys, you got to be ready in every dialect with every shape and form to hex the St. Elmo's fires, the balls of blue light that prowl the earth like sizzling cats. I got the only lightning rods in the 80 worlds that hear, feel, know, and sass back any storm, no matter what tongue, voice, or sign. No foreign thunder so loud this rod can't soft-talk it!'

But Will was staring beyond the man now.

'Which,' he said. 'Which house will it strike?'

'Which? Hold on. Wait.' The salesman searched deep in their faces. 'Some folks draw lightning, suck it like cats suck babies' breath. Some folks' polarities are negative, some positive. Some glow in the dark. Some snuff out. You now, the two. . . I—'

90 'What makes you so sure lightning will strike anywhere around here?' said Jim suddenly, his eyes bright.

The salesman almost flinched. 'Why, I got a nose, an eye, an ear. Both those houses, their timbers! Listen!'

They listened. Maybe their houses leaned under the cool afternoon wind. Maybe not.

'Lightning needs channels, like rivers, to run in. One of those attics is a dry river bottom, itching to let lightning pour through! Tonight!'

'Tonight?' Jim sat up happily.

'No ordinary storm!' said the salesman. 'Tom Fury tells
100 you. Fury, ain't that a fine name for one who sells lightning-rods? Did I take the name? No! Did the name fire me to my occupations? Yes! Grown up, I saw cloudy fires jumping the world, making men hop and hide. Thought: I'll chart hurricanes, map storms, then run ahead shaking iron cudgels, my miraculous defenders, in my fists! I've shielded and made snug-safe one hundred thousand, count 'em, God-fearing homes. So when I tell you, boys, you're in dire need, listen! Climb that roof, nail this rod high, ground it in the good earth before nightfall!'

110 'But which house, which!' asked Will.

The salesman reared off, blew his nose in a great kerchief, then walked slowly across the lawn as if approaching a huge timebomb that ticked silently there.

He touched Will's front porch newels, ran his hand over a post, a floorboard, then shut his eyes and leaned against the house to let its bones speak to him.

Then, hesitant, he made his cautious way to Jim's house next door.

Jim stood up to watch.

120 The salesman put his hand out to touch, to stroke, to quiver his fingertips on the old paint.

'This,' he said at last, 'is the one.'

Jim looked proud.

Without looking back, the salesman said, 'Jim Nightshade, this your place?'

'Mine,' said Jim.

'I should've known,' said the man.

'Hey, what about *me*?' said Will.

The salesman snuffed again at Will's house. 'No, no. Oh, a few sparks'll jump on your rainspouts. But the real show's next door here, at the Nightshades'! Well!'

130   The salesman hurried back across the lawn to seize his huge leather bag.

'I'm on my way. Storm's coming. Don't wait, Jim boy. Otherwise—bamm! You'll be found, your nickels, dimes and Indian-heads fused by electroplating. Abe Lincolns melted into Miss Columbias, eagles plucked raw on the backs of quarters, all run to quicksilver in your jeans. More! Any boy hit by lightning, lift his lid and there on his eyeball, pretty as the Lord's prayer on a pin, find the last scene the boy ever saw! A box-Brownie photo, by God, of that fire climbing down the sky to blow you like a penny whistle, suck your soul back up along the bright stair! Git, boy! Hammer it high or you're dead come dawn!'

And jangling his case full of iron rods, the salesman wheeled about and charged
140 down the walk blinking wildly at the sky, the roof, the trees, at last closing his eyes, moving, sniffing, muttering. 'Yes, bad, here it comes, feel it, way off now, but running fast. . .'

And the man in the storm-dark clothes was gone, his cloud-coloured hat pulled down over his eyes, and the trees rustled and the sky seemed very old suddenly and Jim and Will stood testing the wind to see if they could smell electricity, the lightning-rod fallen between them.

A box-Brownie photo, by God, of that fire climbing down the sky to blow you like a penny whistle, suck your soul back up along the bright stair! Git, boy! Hammer it high or you're dead come dawn!'

150   And jangling his case full of iron rods, the salesman wheeled about and charged down the walk blinking wildly at the sky, the roof, the trees, at last closing his eyes, moving, sniffing, muttering. 'Yes, bad, here it comes, feel it, way off now, but running fast. . .'

And the man in the storm-dark clothes was gone, his cloud-coloured hat pulled down over his eyes, and the trees rustled and the sky seemed very old suddenly and Jim and Will stood testing the wind to see if they could smell electricity, the lightning-rod fallen between them.

by Ray Bradbury

Source 5 |
Extract from
Small Island

About 16,000 West Indians volunteered for service alongside the British during the Second World War, out of the 14-million population of the Caribbean colonies of the British Commonwealth. In this extract, a group of such servicemen stationed in Yorkshire visit the village of Hunmanby.

Now see this, a fine day; a weak, heartless sun resting in a blue sky. We are out of the camp for the first time, six maybe seven of the boys and me. Walking in our RAF blue through the English village of Hunmanby. No order to follow, no command to hear, just us boys. We are remarking on the pretty neatness of the gardens – a flower still in bloom, which someone, I forget who, insists they know the name of. Shutting his eyes and biting his lip he tries to recall it. "A rose," he says.

"Cha, that is not a rose," someone else says. "Every flower is
10 rose to you."

"That is a rose."

"It is not a rose."

This argument is going on as we walk on past the post office and shop. The display in the window, piled up high with tins and boxes, still manages to proclaim that there is a lot of nothing to buy inside. Hubert is trying to persuade James, a strict Presbyterian and teetotal, to come into the pub. "You think one little beer gonna keep you outta heaven?"

It was I who first noticed. Leaning urgently into our group I
20 whispered, "Man, everyone looking at us."

The entire village had come out [...]. Staring out from dusty windows, gawping from shop doors, gaping at the edge of the pavement, craning at gates and peering round corners. The villagers kept their distance but held that gaze of curious trepidation firmly on we West Indian RAF volunteers. Under this scrutiny we darkies moved with the awkwardness of thieves caught in a sunbeam.

"Gilbert, ask them what the problem," Hubert told me.

From every point of the compass eyes were on us. "You have
30 a megaphone for me, man?" I said. When I scratched my head the whole village knew. If any one of those people had a stick long enough, I swear they would have poked us with it.

It was some while before the more daring among them took cautious steps towards us, the unfamiliar. A young woman – curling brunette hair, dark eyes, pretty and plump at the hips – finally stood within an arm's distance to ask, "Are you lot American?" She had her mind on feeling some nylon stockings on her graceful leg. Which, as she stood pert and feminine before us, every one of us boys had our mind on too.

40 "No, we are from Jamaica," I told her.

"The West Indies," the Trinidadian among us corrected.

Like a chink in a dam, the trickle of villagers approached us. Most merely nodded as they passed. An old man with a face as cracked as a dry riverbed shook us all hearty by the hand in turn saying, "We're all in this together, lad. We're glad to have ya."

An elderly couple tapping on James's shoulder asked, "Would you mind, duck – would you mind saying something? Only my husband here says it's not English you're speaking."

50 When James replied, "Certainly, madam, but please tell me what you require me to say," her husband shouted, "Bloody hell, Norma, you're right."

As Norma concluded: "There, I told you. They speak it just like us, only funnier. Ta, ducks, sorry to bother ya."

A middle-aged man, not in uniform, kept his hands resolutely in his pockets before addressing me. Eyeing intently the young woman, who was by now getting on very nicely with a lucky Fulton – consorting with him as we had been assured no white woman would – this man, not looking on my face as

60 he spoke, asked me, "Why would you leave a nice sunny place to come here if you didn't have to?"

When I said, "To fight for my country, sir," his eyebrows jumped like two caterpillars in a polka.

"Humph. Your country?" he asked without need of an answer. He then took the young woman's

70 arm, guiding her, reluctant as she was, away from Fulton and our group.

by Andrea Levy

15

Source 6 | Extract from **The Secret of Crickley Hall**

For many decades James Herbert has terrified his readers. In this short extract he shows how a simple bath can turn into a nightmare experience.

The bath was long enough for Eve to stretch full length, her legs straight, only her head and neck above the waterline. It was almost relaxing lying there cocooned and snug in the warm water, her face wet with light perspiration; only her troubled thoughts kept her from dozing.

She closed her eyes against the starkness of the bathroom with its black and white tiles and plain bowled light overhead. Rain pittered on the frosted window and curls of steam rose from the water in which she tried to relax. The warmth felt good against her skin and her thoughts wandered.

Eve was tired – she always felt tired nowadays, but this week had been particularly
10   stressful. Good idea, Gabe, getting us all away from London so that we wouldn't be at home with its memories on the anniversary of Cam's disappearance, She gave a bitter smile. As if it would make any difference, as if it would hurt any less. But Gabe meant well.

Keeping her eyes closed, she sank lower into the bath, water covering her chin, almost reaching her bottom lip. So warm, so comfortable. Eve began to drift…

Mustn't fall asleep. So tired, though, so wearied by events. And by sorrow. Briefly, she wondered if they would ever find Chester again. lost dog, lost son. The girls were still upset. Over Cam. Over Chester. One loss too many. Sleepy. Very sleepy…

Because her eyes were closed and she was half asleep, Eve didn't at first notice the light above flicker, then dim, then burn out.

20   But she felt the change in temperature that followed almost instantly. It roused her with a start.

The water she bathed in was suddenly chilled – no, it was cold and fast becoming freezing. It was as if it were congealing into ice.

Then, there in the absolute darkness, she heard its sound – ice crackling as it merged on the water's surface.

She lifted her leaden arms and her numbed hands came in contact with the thin icy layer. She pushed against it, but already it was firm and wouldn't break.

Her face, just above the waterline, felt the frigidity of the room itself. Her hair stiffened and crackled with ice particles and the cold beneath seemed to press on her
30   lungs, making it difficult to breath. She tried to call out, but drew in frosted air that constricted her throat. This could not be happening, it was beyond all reason! How could a bath full of heated water freeze over within seconds? It was insane!

The coldness about her body seemed heavy, hardened, and it clamped her limbs, making it almost impossible to move them. And each time she tried to suck in air so that she could scream for help, it was as though a rod of ice had rushed into her throat to stifle any sound, Instead of raising her hands, she pushed them against the bottom of the bath, using her heels too, hoping to break through the glacial surface with her shoulders, but she kept slipping on the porcelain, kept slithering on its slickness.

40 Desperately, she sharply brought up one knee, the foot of the other leg pressed hard against the end of the bath. She heard the ice crack, sensed it give a little, felt the impact on her knee, But the effort caused her head to sink further down into the water, which rushed up her nose and surged into her open mouth. She panicked even more and threw her body around, writhing in the icy thickness, kicking up with both knees now, one after the other, cracking, then breaking the frozen sheet. Her head and shoulders were completely underwater and her back pressed against the bath's solid bottom.

She was frantic, she was terrified. She did not want to drown.

With a massive effort, she lifted her torso, her forehead breaking through the thin layer of ice that was already forming over the opening where her head had been only moments before. She gulped in a huge breath, not caring that it froze her mouth and
50 throat and invaded her lungs like an arctic breeze, just desperate to take in air so that she wouldn't die.

She opened her eyes to the darkness and that was when vice-like fingers clamped the top of her head and pushed her down again. She went under, not understanding, just fighting for her life, tossing herself around, squirming and wriggling, refusing to be still despite the cold, tight embrace of the water, twisting so that the iron hand that held her could not get a firm grip. Eve burst through the surface ice, this time further down in the bath, on leg over the side, the other one bent, her foot pushing against the slippery porcelain.

Blinking to clear her eyes, Eve perceived rather than saw the dark figure looming
60 over her and this time she did scream, for it was an instinctive, animal cry that was not forced but came from sheer terror.

The piercing sound echoed round the tiled bathroom. Now two stunningly gelid hands grasped her, one in her hair, the other on her shoulder. They forced her down once more, but she struggled so much, the ice breaking up completely around her, that they could not keep her under. She heaved herself upwards, screamed again, and the bathroom door crashed open, dismal light from the landing pushing back the reluctant darkness.

Gabe rushed in and grabbed Eve, hauling her out of the bath, hugging her naked shuddering body close. He tried to calm her, squeezing her tight, hushing her sobs with quietly spoken words.

70 'It's all right, Eve, you're safe, I'm here.'

He quickly scanned the room and although it was shadowed, he could tell there was no one else in there.

But he smelt the thick cloying stink of strong soap mixed with decay and excrement.

by James Herbert

Source 7 |
Extract from
The Invisible Man

In the following extract the Invisible Man recounts the first time he went out under the cloak of invisibility. He soon discovers that invisibility is not all that he had hoped it would be. The story was first published in 1897.

"In going downstairs the first time I found an unexpected difficulty because I could not see my feet; indeed I stumbled twice, and there was an unaccustomed clumsiness in gripping the bolt. By not looking down, however, I managed to walk on the level passably well.

"My mood, I say, was one of exaltation. I felt as a seeing man might do, with padded feet and noiseless clothes, in a city of the blind. I experienced a wild impulse to jest, to startle people, to clap men on the back, fling people's hats astray, and

10   generally revel in my extraordinary advantage.

"But hardly had I emerged upon Great Portland Street, however (my lodging was close to the big draper's shop there), when I heard a clashing concussion and was hit violently behind, and turning saw a man carrying a basket of soda-water syphons, and looking in amazement at his burden. Although the blow had really hurt me, I found something so irresistible in his astonishment that I laughed aloud. 'The devil's in the basket,' I said, and suddenly twisted it out of his hand. He let go incontinently, and I swung the whole weight

20   into the air.

"But a fool of a cabman, standing outside a public house, made a sudden rush for this, and his extending fingers took me with excruciating violence under the ear. I let the whole down with a smash on the cabman, and then, with shouts and the clatter of feet about me, people coming out of shops, vehicles pulling up, I realised what I had done for myself, and cursing my folly, backed against a shop window and prepared to dodge out of the confusion. In a moment I should be wedged into a crowd and inevitably discovered. I pushed by a

30   butcher boy, who luckily did not turn to see the nothingness that shoved him aside, and dodged behind the cab-man's four-wheeler. I do not know how they settled the business, I hurried straight across the road, which was happily clear, and hardly heeding which way I went,[...] plunged into the afternoon throng of Oxford Street.

"I tried to get into the stream of people, but they were too thick for me, and in a moment my heels were being trodden upon. I took to the gutter, the roughness of which I found painful to my feet, and forthwith the shaft of a crawling

40   hansom dug me forcibly under the shoulder blade, reminding me that I was already bruised severely. I staggered out of

the way of the cab, avoided a perambulator by a convulsive movement, and found myself behind the hansom. A happy thought saved me, and as this drove slowly along I followed in its immediate wake, trembling and astonished at the turn of my adventure. And not only trembling, but shivering. It was a bright day in January and I was stark naked and the thin slime of mud that covered the road was freezing. Foolish as it seems to me now, I had not reckoned that, transparent or not, I was still amenable to the weather and all its consequences.

"Then suddenly a bright idea came into my head. I ran round and got into the cab. And so, shivering, scared, and sniffling with the first intimations of a cold, and with the bruises in the small of my back growing upon my attention, I drove slowly along Oxford Street and past Tottenham Court Road. My mood was as different from that in which I had sallied forth ten minutes ago as it is possible to imagine. *This* invisibility indeed! The one thought that possessed me was – how was I to get out of the scrape I was in.

"We crawled past Mudie's, and there a tall woman with five or six yellow-labelled books hailed my cab, and I sprang out just in time to escape her, shaving a railway van narrowly in my flight. I made off up the roadway to Bloomsbury Square, intending to strike north past the museum and so get into the quiet district. I was now cruelly chilled, and the strangeness of my situation so unnerved me that I whimpered as I ran. At the northward corner of the Square a little white dog ran out of the Pharmaceutical Society's offices, and incontinently made for me, nose down.

"I had never realised it before, but the nose is to the mind of a dog what the eye is to the mind of a seeing man. Dogs perceive the scent of a man moving as men perceive his vision. This brute began barking and leaping, showing, as it seemed to me, only too plainly that he was aware of me. I crossed Great Russell Street, glancing over my shoulder as I did so, and went some way along Montague Street before I realised what I was running towards.

"Then I became aware of a blare of music, and looking along the street saw a number of people advancing out of Russell Square, red shirts, and the banner of the Salvation Army to the fore. Such a crowd, chanting in the roadway

and scoffing on the pavement, I could not hope to penetrate, and dreading to go back and farther from home again, and deciding on the spur of the moment, I ran up the white steps of a house facing the museum railings, and stood there until the crowd should have passed. Happily the dog stopped at the noise of the band too, hesitated, and turned tail, running back to Bloomsbury Square again.

...

90 "Thud, thud, thud, came the drum of the band, [...] and for the moment I did not notice two urchins stopping at the railings by me. 'See 'em,' said one. 'See what?' said the other. 'Why – them footmarks – *bare*. Like what you makes in mud.'

"I looked down and saw the youngsters had stopped and were gaping at the muddy footmarks I had left behind me up the newly whitened steps.[...] 'There's a barefoot man gone up them steps, or I don't know nothing,' said one. 'And he ain't never come down again. And his foot was a-bleeding.'

"The thick of the crowd had already passed. 'Looky here, 100 Ted,' quoth the younger of the detectives, with the sharpness of surprise in his voice, and pointed straight to my feet. I looked

down and saw at once the dim suggestion of their outline sketched in splashes of mud. For a moment I was paralysed.

"'Why, that's rum,' said the elder. 'Dashed rum! It's just like the ghost of a foot, ain't it?' He hesitated and advanced with outstretched hand. A man pulled up short to see what he was catching, and then a girl. In another moment he would have touched me. Then I saw what to do. I made a step, the boy started back with an exclamation, and with a rapid movement
110 I swung myself over into the portico of the next house. But the smaller boy was sharp-eyed enough to follow the movement, and before I was well down the steps and upon the pavement, he had recovered from his momentary astonishment and was shouting out that the feet had gone over the wall.

"They rushed round and saw my new footmarks flash into being on the lower step and upon the pavement. 'What's up?' asked someone. 'Feet! Look! Feet running!' Everybody in the road, except my three pursuers, was pouring along after the Salvation Army, and this blow not only impeded me but
120 them. There was an eddy of surprise and interrogation. At the cost of bowling over one young fellow I got through, and in another moment I was rushing headlong round the circuit of Russell Square, with six or seven astonished people following my footmarks. There was no time for explanation, or else the whole host would have been after me.

"Twice I doubled round corners, thrice I crossed the road and came back upon my tracks, and then, as my feet grew hot and dry, the damp impressions began to fade. At last I had a breathing space and rubbed my feet clean with my hands,
130 and so got away altogether. The last I saw of the chase was a little group of a dozen people perhaps, studying with infinite perplexity a slowly drying footprint that had resulted from a puddle in Tavistock Square, – a footprint as isolated and incomprehensible to them as Crusoe's solitary discovery."

by H. G. Wells

Source 8 | On The Sidewalk Bleeding

Through the thoughts and feelings of a young gang member, Andy, Evan Hunter reveals the bitter side of gang life in New York.

The boy lay on the sidewalk bleeding in the rain. He was sixteen years old, and he wore a bright purple jacket, and the lettering across the back of the jacket read THE ROYALS. The boy's name was Andy and the name was delicately scripted in black thread on the front of the jacket, just over the heart. ANDY.

He had been stabbed ten minutes ago. The knife entered just below his rib cage and had been drawn across his body violently, tearing a wide gap in his flesh. He lay on the sidewalk with the March rain drilling his jacket and drilling his body and washing away the blood that poured from his open wound. He had known excruciating pain when the knife had torn across his body, and then sudden comparative relief when the

10 blade was pulled away. He had heard the voice saying, "That's for you Royal!" and then the sound of footsteps hurrying into the rain.

He tried to yell for help, but he had no voice. He did not know why his voice had deserted him, or why there was an open hole in his body from which his life ran readily, steadily, or why the rain had become so suddenly fierce. It was 11:13 p.m. but he did not know the time.

There was another thing he did not know.

He did not know he was dying. He lay on the sidewalk, bleeding, and he thought only: that was a fierce rumble. They got me good that time, but he did not know he was dying. He would have been frightened had he known. In his ignorance he lay bleeding and

20 wishing he could cry out for help, but there was no voice in his throat. There was only the bubbling of blood from between his lips whenever he opened his mouth to speak.

He could hear the sound of automobile tyres hushed on the rain swept streets, far away at the other end of the long alley. He lay with his face pressed to the sidewalk, and he could see the splash of neon far away at the other end of the alley, tinting the pavement red and green, slickly brilliant in the rain.

He wondered if Laura would be angry. He had left the jump to get a pack of cigarettes. He had told her he would be back in a few minutes, and then he had gone downstairs and found the candy store closed. He knew that Alfredo's on the next block would be open. He had started through the alley, and that was when he had been ambushed.

30 He could hear the faint sound of music now, coming from a long, long way off. He wondered if Laura was dancing, wondered if she had missed him yet. He thought of her face, the brown eyes and the jet-black hair, and thinking of her he forgot his pain a little.

The couple came into the alley suddenly. They ran into the alley together, running from the rain. Andy watched them run into the alley laughing, and then duck into the doorway not ten feet from him.

"Man, what rain!" the boy said. "You could drown out there."

"I have to get home," the girl said. "It's late, Freddie. I have to get home."

"We got time," Freddie said. "Your people won't raise a fuss if you're a little late."

"It's dark," the girl said, and she giggled.

40 "Yeah," the boy answered, his voice very low.

There was a long silence. Then the girl said, "Oh," only that single word, and Andy knew she had been kissed, and he suddenly hungered for Laura's mouth. It was then that he wondered if he would ever kiss Laura again. It was then that he wondered if he was dying.

"I love you, Angela," the boy said.

"I love you, too, Freddie," the girl said, and Andy listened and thought: I love you, Laura. Laura, I think maybe I'm dying. Laura, this is stupid but I think maybe I'm dying.

He tried to speak. He tried to move. He tried to crawl toward the doorway. He tried to make a noise, a sound, and a grunt came, a low animal grunt of pain.

50 "What was that?" the girl said, suddenly alarmed, breaking away from the boy.

Andy moved his lips again. Again the sound came from him.

"I'll go see," the boy said.

He stepped into the alley. He walked over to where Andy lay on the ground. He stood over him, watching him.

"You all right?" he asked.

"What is it?" Angela said from the doorway.

"Somebody's hurt," Freddie said.

"Let's get out of here," Angela said.

"No. Wait a minute." He knelt down beside Andy. "You cut?" he asked.

60 Andy nodded. The boy kept looking at him. He saw the lettering on the jacket then. THE ROYALS. He turned to Angela.

"He's a Royal," he said. "We help him, and the Guardians'll be down on our necks."

"Is he . . . is he hurt bad?"

"Yeah, it looks that way."

"What shall we do?"

"I don't know. If we get a cop, the Guardians'll find out who," Freddie said.

Angela hesitated a long time. Then she said, "I want to go home, Freddie. My people will begin to worry."

"Yeah," Freddie said. Andy lifted his face from the sidewalk, and his eyes said: Please, please help me, and maybe Freddie read what his eyes were saying, and maybe he didn't.

He looked at Andy again, and then mumbled, "I'm sorry." He took Angela's arm and together they ran towards the neon splash at the other end of the alley.

Why, they're afraid of the Guardians, Andy thought in amazement. But why should they be? I wasn't afraid of the Guardians. I never turkeyed out of a rumble with the Guardians. I got heart. But I'm bleeding.

The rain was soothing somehow. It was a cold rain, but his body was hot all over, and the rain helped cool him. He had always liked rain. He could remember sitting in Laura's house one time, the rain running down the windows, and just looking out over the street, watching the people running from the rain. That was when he'd first joined the Royals.

He could remember how happy he was when the Royals had taken him. The Royals and the Guardians, two of the biggest. He was a Royal. There had been meaning to the title.

Now, in the alley, with the cold rain washing his hot body, he wondered about the meaning. If he died, he was Andy. He was not a Royal. He was simply Andy, and he was dead. And he wondered suddenly if the Guardians who had ambushed him and knifed him had ever once realized he was Andy? Had they known that he was Andy or had they simply known that he was a Royal wearing a purple silk jacket?

I'm Andy, he screamed wordlessly, I'm Andy.

90   An old lady stopped at the other end of the alley. The garbage cans were stacked there, beating noisily in the rain. The old lady carried an umbrella with broken ribs, carried it like a queen. She stepped intothe mouth of the alley, shopping bag over one arm. She lifted the lids of the garbage cans. She did not hear Andy grunt because she was a little deaf and because the rain was beating on the cans. She collected her string and her newspapers, and an old hat with a feather on it from one of the garbage cans, and a broken footstool from another of the cans. And then she replaced the lids and lifted her umbrella high and walked out the alley mouth. She has worked quickly and soundlessly, and now she was gone.

    The alley looked very long now. He could see people passing at the other end of it,
100 and he wondered who the people were, and he wondered if he would ever get to know them, wondered who it was of the Guardians who had plunged the knife into his body.

    "That's for you, Royal!" the voice had said. Even in his pain, there had been some sort of pride in knowing he was a Royal. Now there was no pride at all. With the rain beginning to chill him, with the blood pouring steadily between his fingers, he knew only a sort of dizziness. He could only think: I want to be Andy.

    He felt weak and very tired. He knew he was going to die now. He was filled with sadness that his life would be over at sixteen. He felt all at once as if he had never done anything, never seen anything, never been anywhere. There were so many things to do. He wondered why he'd never thought of them before, wondered why the rumbles and
110 the jumps and the purple jackets had always seemed so important to him before. Now they seemed like such small things in a world he was missing, a world that was rushing past at the other end of the alley.

    It seemed very important to him that he take off the purple jacket. He was very close to dying, and when they found him, he did not want them to say, "Oh, it's a Royal." With great effort, he rolled over onto his back. He felt the pain tearing at his stomach when he moved. If he never did another thing, he wanted to take off the jacket. The jacket had only one meaning now. If he had not been wearing the jacket, he wouldn't have been stabbed. The knife had not been plunged in hatred of Andy. The knife hated only the purple jacket. The jacket was a stupid meaningless thing that was robbing him of his life.

120   He lay struggling with the shiny wet jacket. His arms were heavy. Pain ripped fire across his body whenever he moved. But he squirmed and fought and twisted until one arm was free and then the other. He rolled away from the jacket and lay quite still, breathing heavily, listening to the sound of his breathing and the sounds of the rain and thinking: Rain is sweet, I'm Andy.

by Evan Hunter

Source 9 | The Photograph

In this story Sefi Atta unites her homeland of Africa with her current home of America through a startling exposé of contrasting attitudes to food.

Picture her: a girl with hollow cheeks and sunken eyes; her dress hangs off her shoulders. Dust spirals above her in the aftermath of the relief trucks. Their huge tyre marks on the dry ground are all that's left of the mission to her village. The sun is at its hottest; the African sky endless and merciless. Even the white men with cameras, clicking away to capture the usual scrimmage over food deliveries, are hopping into their jeeps, and speeding off to an air-conditioned hotel in a city miles away. They are photojournalists.

10 One of them, sun-burned and drenched in sweat, dressed in a khaki shirt and jeans, kneels to take a photograph of the girl before he leaves. In his breast pocket is a melted protein bar, as untouched as his conscience. He is not responsible for the cruelty of nature, or the incompetence of governments. And who really can tolerate the stench of human waste in a ditch nearby, unless they have no choice but to live in a place like this?

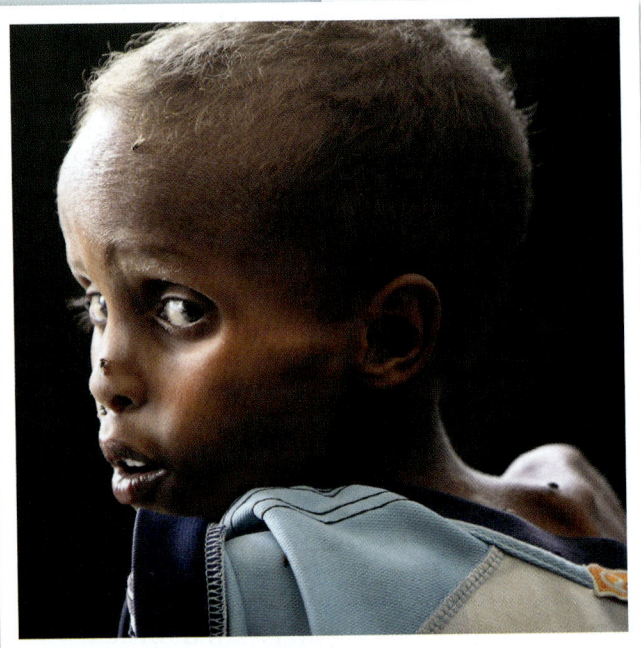

Professionally, the girl caught his attention. She was surrounded by a group of boys, and she seemed just 20 as determined as they scrambled when the relief trucks arrived. She was pushed down and trampled on. When she found her feet, the sacks of grain had already been dragged away. She remained there, red-eyed, and stroking the earth with her fingertips.

The journalist takes his final shot, returns to America with several reels of film. His photograph 30 of the girl sells and is placed on the front cover of a magazine for current affairs. He receives accolades and gains enemies among his colleagues. He changes his girlfriend for one who thinks he is under-appreciated and cavalier. "You've captured the face of hunger in Africa," his editor summarizes about the photograph, and he stops himself from reminding the man that this photograph is just one face, in one village in Africa. Still, he benefits from the praise, and the recognition for 40 his work, at last.

The photograph is in most newsstands by month end, even in the bookstore of a mall in America that people visit to peruse bestsellers and magazines with no intention of buying them. They look at the face of the African girl and quickly turn away to salvage their shopping sprees. But they are struck by her image, like one teenager who has finished flipping through the latest copy of Vogue. She notices the photograph under the heading 'Drought in Africa'. Her parents are from that continent. She herself was born and 50 bred in America, raised on Disney and has never travelled out. She is embarrassed by such images. They remind her of her classmates who joke about starving Africans. She isn't African that way, or American in an apple pie way either.

When she was a girl, Cinderella, Snow White and all the other Disney princesses didn't resemble her. When she became interested in fashion, neither did the cover models. Then, it seemed the magazines discovered Africa had beautiful women. 60 There was the model from Sudan who, supposedly, was once a refugee; there was the Nigerian model who was discovered in the Miss Africa pageant.

This Nigerian model is in the latest copy of Vogue, dressed in linen, and thin, so thin the teenager is conscious of her own hips. She thinks she is too fat. She wants to wear jeans that cling to her bones like skin. She would love to be photographed with aloof 70 eyes like the Nigerian model. She diets on protein shakes and secretly sticks her finger down her throat to vomit. And it doesn't matter what reasons there are for a world where some people starve, while others starve themselves. The hunger that consumes her is real, so she stares at the girl in photograph, ignores the background of drought, and admires her cheek bones.

by Sefi Atta

Source 10 | A Sunrise on the Veldt

The 'veldt' is a term used to define certain wide open rural spaces of Southern Africa. In the start of this short story, a boy ventures out into the early morning with only his dogs and his gun.

Every night that winter he said aloud into the dark of the pillow: Half-past four! Half-past four! till he felt his brain had gripped the words and held them fast. Then he fell asleep at once, as if a shutter had fallen; and lay with his face turned to the clock so that he could see it first thing when he woke.

It was half-past four to the minute, every morning. Triumphantly pressing down the alarm knob of the clock, which the dark half of his mind had outwitted, remaining vigilant all night and counting the hours as he lay relaxed in sleep, he huddled down for a last warm moment under the clothes, playing with the idea of lying abed for this once only. But he played with it for the fun of knowing that it was a weakness that he could
10 defeat without effort; just as he set the alarm each night for the delight of the moment when he awoke and stretched his limbs, feeling the muscles tighten, and thought: Even my brain – even that! I can control every part of myself.

Luxury of warm rested body, with the arms and legs and fingers waiting like soldiers for a word of command! Joy of knowing that the precious hours were given to sleep voluntarily! – for he had once stayed awake three nights running, to prove that he could, and then worked all day, refusing even to admit that he was tired; and now sleep seemed to him a servant to be commanded and refused.

The boy stretched his frame full-length, touching the wall at his head with his hands, and the bed foot with his toes; then he sprung out, like a fish leaping from water.
20 And it was cold, cold.

He always dressed rapidly, so as to try and conserve his night-warmth till the sun rose two hours later; but by the time he had on his clothes his hands were numbed and he could scarcely hold his shoes. These he could not put on for fear of waking his parents, who never came to know how early he rose.

As soon as he stepped over the lintel, the flesh of his soles contracted on the chill earth, and his legs began to ache with cold. It was night: the stars were glittering, the trees standing black and still. He looked for signs of day, for the greying of the edge of a stone, or a lightening in the sky where the sun would rise, but there was nothing yet. Alert as an animal he crept past the dangerous window, standing poised with his hand
30 on the sill for one proudly fastidious moment, looking in at the stuffy blackness of the room where his parents lay.

Feeling for the grass edge of the path with his toes, he reached inside another window further along the wall, where his gun had been set in readiness the night before. The steel was icy, and numbed fingers slipped along it, so that he had to hold it in the crook of his arm for safety. Then he tiptoed to the room where the dogs slept, fearful that they might have been tempted to go before him; but they were waiting, their haunches crouched in reluctance at the cold, but ears and swinging tails greeting the gun ecstatically. His warning undertone kept them secret and silent till the house was a hundred yards back: then they bolted off into the bush, yelping excitedly. The boy
40 imagined his parents turning in their beds and muttering: Those dogs again! before they were dragged back in sleep; and he smiled scornfully. He always looked back over his shoulder at the house before he passed a wall of trees that shut it from sight. It looked so low and small, crouching there under a tall and brilliant sky. Then he turned his back on it, and on the frowsting sleepers, and forgot them.

He would have to hurry. Before the light grew strong he must be four miles away; and already a tint of green stood in the hollow of a leaf, and the air smelled of morning and the stars were dimming.

by Doris Lessing

Source 11 | The Evening Gift

In this complete short story, Sankar is faced with a moral dilemma: should he stay or go?

He had a most curious occupation in life. Having failed in every effort, he had to accept it with gratitude and enthusiasm; he received thirty rupees a month for it. He lived on fifteen rupees in a cheap hotel, where he was given a sort of bunk in the loft, with rafters touching his head. He saved fifteen rupees for paying off the family loan in the village incurred over his sister's marriage. He added a rupee or two to his income by filling money order forms and postcards for unlettered villagers, whom he met on the post office veranda. But his main work was very odd. His business consisted in keeping a wealthy drunkard company. This wealthy man wanted someone to check his drink after nine in the evening, and take him home. Sankar's physique qualified him for this

10 task. 'Don't hesitate to use force on me if necessary,' his employer had told him. But it was never done. Sankar did all that he could by persuasion and it was a quite familiar sight at the Oriental Cafe Bar – the wrangling going on between the employer and his servant. But Sankar with a margin of five minutes always succeeded in wresting the gentleman from his cups and pushing him into his car. On the following morning he was asked: 'What time did we reach home last night?'

'Nine fifteen, sir –'

'Nine fifteen! – Very good, very good. I'm glad. On no account should you let me stay on beyond nine, even if I am in company –'

'Yes, sir.'

20 'You may go now, and be sure to be back in the evening in time –'

That finished his morning duty. He went back to his garret, slept part of the day, loitered about post offices, courts, etc., and returned to work at six o'clock.

'Come on,' said his employer, who waited for him on the veranda, and Sankar got into the front seat of the car and they drove off to the Oriental Cafe.

Today he was in a depressed state, he felt sick of his profession, the perpetual cajoling and bullying, the company of a drunkard. He nearly made up his mind to throw up this work and go back to the village. A nostalgia for his home and people seized him. 'I don't care what happens, I will get back home and do something else to earn this money.' On top of this mood a letter from home: 'Send a hundred rupees

30 immediately. Last date for mortgage instalment. Otherwise we shall lose our house –' He was appalled! Where could he find the money? What was the way out? He cursed his lot more than ever. He sat for a long time thinking of a way out.[…] It was their last possession in this world. If it went, his mother, brothers, and his little sister would have to wander about without a roof over their heads. But could he find a hundred rupees?

What did they mean by putting it off till the last momemt? He cursed his lot for being the eldest son of a troubled family.

He swung into duty as usual. He held the curtain apart for his master as he entered the cubicle. He pressed a bell. He might be a machine, doing this thing for thirty days in the month for nearly twelve months now. The waiter appeared. No talk was necessary. Sankar nodded. The waiter went away and returned a few minutes later with an unopened flat bottle, a soda, and a glass tumbler; placed these on the table and withdrew. [...]

Now Sankar's business would be to pour out a measure of drink into the tumbler, push it up, and place the soda near at hand, go out on to the veranda, and read a newspaper there (with the flat bottle in his pocket), and stay there till he was called in again to fill the glass. By about ten to nine the last ounce of drink would be poured out, and Sankar would sit down opposite to his master instead of going out to the veranda. This was a sort of warning bell.

'Why do you sit here? Go to the veranda.'

'I like this place, sir, and I will sit here.'

'It is not time for you to come in yet.'

'Just ten minutes more, sir.'

'Nonsense. It is just seven o'clock.'

'About two hours ago –'

'You people seem to turn up the clock just as you like – let me see how much is left in the bottle –'

'Nothing,' Sankar said, holding up the empty bottle. 'The last drop was poured out.' He held up the bottle and the other became furious at the sight of it. 'I think,' he said with deep suspicion, 'there is some underhand transaction going on – I don't know what you have been doing in the veranda with the bottle –' Sankar learnt not to answer these charges. As the clock struck nine, he tapped the other's shoulder and said, 'Please finish your drink and get up, sir –' 'What do you mean by it? I'm not getting up. Who are you to order me?'

Sankar had to be firm.

'Look here, don't you be a fool and imagine I am talking in drink. I am dead sober – leave me alone.'

Sankar persisted.

'I dismiss you today, you are no longer in my service. I don't want a disobedient fool for a companion, get out –' Usually Sankar sat through it without replying, and when the drink was finished he gently pulled the other up and led the way to the car, and the other followed, scowling at him with red eyes and abusing him wildly. Today when his employer said, 'I dismiss you, get out this minute –' Sankar replied, 'How can you dismiss me all of a sudden! Must I starve?'

'No. I will give you four months' salary if you get out this moment.' Sankar thought over it.

'Don't sit there. Make up your mind quickly –' said his master. One hundred and twenty rupees! Twenty rupees more than the debt. He could leave for his village and give the cash personally to his mother, and leave his future to God. He brushed aside this vision, shook his head and said: 'No, sir. You have got to get up now, sir.' 'Get out of
80 my service –' shouted his master. He rang the bell and shouted for the waiter, 'Get me another –' Sankar protested to the waiter. 'Get out of here –' cried his master. 'You think I'm speaking in drink. I don't want you. I can look after myself. If you don't leave me, I will tell the waiter to neck you out –' Sankar stood baffled. 'Now, young man –' He took out his wallet: 'What is your salary?'

'Thirty rupees, sir.'

'Here's your four-months. Take it and be off. I have some business meeting here, and I will go home just when I like, there is the car.' He held out a hundred-rupee note and two tens. Mortgage instalment. How can I take it? A conflict raged in Sankar's mind, and he finally took the money and said : 'Thank you very much, sir.'

90 'Don't mention it.[...] Just ordinary duty, that is all. My principle is "Do unto others as you would be done by others" ... You need not come in the morning. I've no need for you. I had you only as a temporary arrangement I'll put in a word for you if any friend wants a clerk or something of the sort –'

'Good-bye, sir.'

'Good-bye.' He was gone. The gentleman looked after him with satisfaction, muttering: 'My principle is ... unto other ...'

Next morning Sankar went out shopping, purchased bits of silk for his younger sister, a pair of spectacles for his mother and a few painted tin toys for the child at home. He went to the hotel, looked into the accounts, and settled his month's bill. 'I'm
100 leaving today,' he said. 'I am returning to my village . . .' His heart was all aflame with joy. He paid a rupee to the servant as tip. He packed up his trunk and bed, took a last look round his garret. [...] He was at the bus stand at about eleven in the day. The bus was ready to start. He took his seat. He would be at home at six in the evening. What a surprise for his mother! He would chat all night and tell them about the drunkard ...

He was shaken out of this reverie. A police inspector standing at the foot-board of the bus touched his shoulder and asked:

'Are you Sankar?'

'Yes.'

'Get down and follow me.'

110 'I am going to my village ...'

'You can't go now.' The inspector placed the trunk and bed on a coolie's head and they marched to the police station. There Sankar was subjected to much questioning, and his pockets were searched and all his money was taken away by the inspector. The inspector scrutinized the hundred-rupee note and remarked: 'Same number. How did you get this? Be truthful …'

Presently the inspector got up and said: 'Follow me to the gentleman's house …' Sankar found his employer sitting in a chair in the veranda, with a very tired look on his face. He motioned the inspector to a chair and addressed Sankar in a voice full of sorrow. 'I never knew you were this sort, Sankar. You robbed me when I was not aware of it. If you'd asked me I'd have given you any amount you wanted. Did you have to tie me up and throw me down?' He showed the bruises on his arm. 'In addition to robbing?' Sankar stood aghast. He could hardly speak for trembling. He explained all that had happened in the evening. His master and the police inspector listened in grim silence with obvious scepticism. His master said to the inspector: 'Can you believe anything of what he says?'

120

'No, sir,' replied the inspector.

'Nor can I. The poor fellow is driven to a corner and is inventing things ...' He thought for a moment. 'I don't know ... I think ... since you have recovered the amount ... how much
130 did you find with him?'

'About one hundred and ten rupees and some change ...' said the inspector.

'What happened to the balance?' He turned to Sankar and asked:

'Did you spend it?'

'Yes, I bought some toys and clothes ...'

'Well, well,' said the gentleman with a flourish. 'Let it go, poor devil: I'm sorry for you. You could have asked me for the money instead of robbing me by force. Do you know where
140 they found me?' he asked, showing the bruises on his elbow. 'Do you know it was nearly next day they took me home? You'd left me unconscious: I will, however, withdraw my complaint. "Do unto others as you would be done by" is my motto. You have served me faithfully all these months ... but don't come before me again, you are a rogue. Get away now ...'

'Inspector, after the formalities are over you may send me the seized amount tomorrow, thank you very much ...'

Sankar starved for two days, and wandered about the street without a place for his head or trunk. At last, loitering near the
150 post office one day, he had a few money orders and postcards to write, which earned him a rupee. With it he ate a meal, and took the bus for his village and back to all the ancient never-ending troubles of his family life.

by R. K. Narayan

Literary Non-Fiction

What is literary non-fiction?

To many, the term non-fiction suggests facts: things that are known to have actually happened. The contents of an encyclopaedia can be classed as non-fiction, being an assortment of facts on a range of topics. However, the category 'literary non-fiction' contains a much broader range of texts than can be found in an encyclopaedia. It includes travel and adventure writing, autobiography, biography, diaries, discursive writing, and much more. These genres are all based on fact but they are very different from an entry in an encyclopaedia.

The Voice of the Writer

The things that are described or recounted in literary non-fiction did happen. Unlike the imaginary worlds of fiction, the people, places, events and characters are based on reality: actual people, identifiable places, real events. But – and this is an important 'but' to remember – they are presented to the reader through the perceptions and voice of the writer. Try asking five people to describe the same event; you will find that you have five very different descriptions. They will see, hear, think and feel different things. It is the same with many kinds of non-fiction. It is the perceptions and voice of the writer, and his or her skills in writing, that colour and enhance the facts contained within the account, and that make us want to read on.

Discovering the Qualities

There is, therefore, a clear overlap between the techniques used in the fiction texts in Section A and several of the non-fiction texts contained in this section. Many of the writers here use the narrative form – they present their accounts as though they were telling a story, albeit a story based on fact. They use language to paint pictures of real people, real places and real events. In many cases, the writer speaks directly to the reader, often reflecting on the events described and giving an opinion on these. For instance, in the extract from *Tickling the English*, Dara O Briain reflects on a recent gig, while in the extract from *Getups,* Maya Angelou expresses direct opinions on the desirability or otherwise of fashion.

As with fiction, there is a great variety of non-fiction texts in the world. This selection will give you a taste of the wide range of texts available to you which you can enjoy and learn from.

Source 1 | The Beggar King

Aminatta Forna is an author and television documentary maker. In the following extract she tells of how an anxious wait in an airport in Sierra Leone is made bearable by the presence of a young street performer.

The crowd was growing. We began to fear being overtaken by numbers so rose and joined the crush at the gate. A woman next to me wept silently, her head bowed as the tears poured out of her. Sierra Leone had been a country where public tears never failed to attract the sympathy of strangers but nobody put out a hand to comfort her. I'm afraid to say I behaved no differently. Among so many sad souls, what was one more? The minutes passed. The young woman wept on.

Then at the rear of the crowd, came a man's voice, calling
10 loudly: "So, here you are. What are you doing here?" People kept their faces averted, locked in the act of willing the plane to land. "Come home," he boomed. "Come home with me." I am guessing at what he said, because at first I wasn't listening to the words and nor had I turned to look at him. But somebody nearby tittered and this caught my attention.

"Please, I beg you." I turned around and saw a young man: slim, dressed in a plain white cotton robe with a white embroidered round hat. He looked as though he was on his way to the mosque. He was strikingly handsome: bright-eyed
20 and burnished of skin, with dimples in his cheeks.

"Don't leave me. Don't go away. Whatever I have done we can make better. I will change. I can become a different man." Now he had caught our attention. People craned their necks to see who he was talking to, murmured and whispered.

The handsome young man racked it up a notch: "If you get on the plane you'll be taken away from me forever. If you go to America, you'll never come back. Take me with you." He was addressing the weeping woman, speaking his words to her back. By now people were openly curious. The young man
30 continued: "That other woman means nothing to me." And as an afterthought: "Well, not a great deal."

A burst of laughter from the crowd. Suddenly we realised we were watching a street performer, who had picked as his victim the weeping girl. He shook his head and continued: "But the other three, they meant very little. And as for the rest, nothing at all!"

The crowd hooted. The young man had us laughing, but it seemed unfair to pick on this unhappy young woman. Her head was bowed, her shoulders continued to shake. With the back

40 of her hand she wiped away her tears. The street performer dropped to his knees and spread his arms: "See how I beg you. Look at me, I won't move until you give me just one glance."

Everyone looked at the girl, whose back remained turned. I looked at her too. Then I saw the shaking of her shoulders no longer came from sadness, but from laughter. She was helplessly crying and laughing as one. Slowly she lifted her head, turned and faced the young man. Her face was soaked with tears, but she smiled.

We went wild.

50 Footsteps, a shout: the manager of the airport building. He was angry, on the brink of rage. He gestured threateningly at the young man, who leapt to his feet, took his hat from his head and passed it into the crowd. Delayed by a locked gate and hampered by an impossibly large bunch of keys, the manager swore, raised his fist and proceeded to give vigorous chase as the young man danced through the crowd. We closed around him and at the same time passed his hat from hand to hand, stuffing it with money.

When he had made his way to the edge of the crowd the
60 young man made a run for it. Soon enough the manager broke free of us too. Now they were out in the open. The manager charged. The young man skipped out of range. Somebody held out his hat. The young man darted sideways to receive it. The manager lumbered after him, an ox in pursuit of a cat. Rage had the better of him. He screamed at the young man and at us, too. He would not tolerate beggars outside the airport building. The young man, by now standing atop a low wall shouted: "I am a beggar, true. But am I not the King of Beggars?" It was very Errol Flynn.

70 There was much cheering and clapping. The Beggar King bowed, leapt from the wall and was gone. An hour later a plane landed. We boarded it and left, some among us forever.

by Aminatta Forna

Source 2 | Extract from **Work your Way Around the World**

Susan Griffith is a freelance editor and writer who has specialized in writing books and articles about travel. In the following extract she offers advice on the subject of working abroad.

Short of emigrating or marrying a native, working abroad is the best way of experiencing a foreign culture from the inside. The plucky Briton who spends a few months on a Queensland cattle station will have a different tale to tell about Australia from the one who serves behind the bar in a Sydney pub. Yet both will experience the exhilaration of doing something completely unfamiliar in an alien setting.

Working abroad is one of the means by which it is possible to stay overseas for an extended period, to have a chance to get below the surface of a foreign culture, to meet foreign people on their own terms and to gain a better perspective on your own culture and habits. The kind of job you find will determine the stratum of society in which you

10 will mix and therefore the content of the experience. The traveller who spends a few weeks picking olives for a Cretan farmer will get a very different insight into the life and times of modern Greece from the traveller who looks after the children of a wealthy Athenian shipping magnate. And both will probably have more culturally worthwhile experiences than the traveller who settles for working at a beach café frequented only by his or her partying compatriots.

Anyone with a taste for adventure and a modicum of nerve has the potential for exploring far-flung corners of the globe on very little money. In an ideal world, it would be possible to register with an international employment agency and wait to be assigned to a glamorous job as an underwater photography model in the Caribbean,

20 history co-ordinator for a European tour company or ski tow operator in New Zealand. But jobs abroad, like jobs at home, must be ferreted out. The internet has had an enormous impact and those prepared to surf can make their way through the deluge of information to specific job listings overseas.

At the risk of oversimplifying the range of choices, the aspiring working traveller either fixes up a definite job before leaving home or takes a gamble on finding something on the spot. There is a lot to recommend prior planning, especially to people – students taking a gap year for instance – who have never travelled abroad and who feel some trepidation at the prospect.

A range of mediating organisations and agencies exist and can offer advice and

30 practical assistance to those who wish to fix up a job before leaving home. Some accept a tiny handful of individuals who satisfy stringent requirements, others accept almost anyone who can pay the required fee. For example, various agencies arrange for large numbers of young people to spend the summer working at children's summer camps in the US, as English teachers in Eastern Europe and as volunteers on Israeli *kibbutzim*. Students occupy a privileged position since a number of schemes are open only to them

and student exchange organisations can help with the nitty-gritty of arranging work abroad… for example BUNAC (British Universities North America Club) has a choice of programmes in the US, Canada, Jamaica, Australia, New Zealand, South Africa, Ghana and, most recently, Argentina…

40   True 'working holidays' are rare, though they do exist. For example, travellers have exchanged their labour for a free trip with an outback Australian camping tour operator or on a cruise to the midnight sun. But in most cases, the expression 'working holiday' is an oxymoron in the same way as 'cruel kindness'. Jobs are jobs wherever you do them. There is seldom scope for swanning around art galleries, cafes and clubs if you are picking grapes seven days a week. Sometimes the most distasteful jobs of all are the ones that allow you to save quickly to finance the next leg of your journey.

Those who shed their unrealistic expectations are normally exhilarated by the novelty and challenge of working abroad. Any individual with guts and gusto, whether a student or a grandmother, has the potential of funding him or herself to various
50   corners of the globe. Persistence, optimism and resilience are the only ingredients essential for such a venture.

by Susan Griffith

Source 3 | Fall of Antwerp, October 1914

A soldier recounts his battalion's venture into the besieged port of Antwerp, recalling a moment of humanity in a world of war.

On a brisk October morning we arrived in the threatened port of Antwerp. The people lined the street, they cheered, they waved, there were flowers and wine. The war was young and so were we. We felt gallant, they felt relieved. Out to the trenches we went. We settled, opened reserve ammunition, fixed our bayonets and said, "Now let 'em come!"

Night came but not the enemy. We posted sentries and settled down, but not for long. Heavy rifle fire broke out on the left, then on the right. We manned the firing step and peered over. Searchlights from the fort swept the front. We could see nothing. We held our fire and felt neglected.

10 Morning came but still no enemy. Suddenly high in the sky was a train-like rumble and whistle followed by an explosion. Smoke and flame shot up in the city. An old hand said, "Them's howitzer shells. The bastards must be a dozen miles away."

At intervals throughout the day these rumbling shells rolled over, flames shooting up after each explosion. Then the oil tanks by the dockside were alight. The smoke gathered over the port to join the autumn mists and the glow from the fires. It looked like hell. We could only wait. We felt useless.

On the 8th of October an order came, "Prepare to move." Just at the back of our trench was a deserted farm. Odd men had gone scrounging in the farm and as were about to move, an officer shouted to me, "Sergeant, see the farm's clear." Coming back 20 through an outhouse, I saw some pails of milk and I did a most unsoldierly action. I emptied my half-full water-bottle and filled it full of milk. We soon got orders to move to the right and onto the road and we thought, "Ah, they won't come to us. We're going out to them."

On reaching the road, instead of turning left to the enemy, we turned right to the city and we received the most deadening, soul-racking order a soldier can receive. Retreat. We picked our way through the burning buildings, past the flaming oil tanks to the flaming pontoon bridge the engineers had build for us to cross and then destroy. On each side of the bridge stood hordes of refugees of every kind – children, women, nuns, priests. This was the bridge of sighs. They had been stopped so we could cross. The flare 30 from the burning lit their faces, expressionless and hopeless, and we felt ashamed. An officer called to me, 'Sergeant! Shout "Break Step!"' It should have been "Break Hearts!"

We were soon across and in open country. After a few miles we arrived at a Belgian village, marched into a cobbled square, and the orders were, "Rest where you stand. Be ready for any alarm."

"Sad" is not a soldier's word – browned off, fed up, yes, but the only time a solider is really and deeply sad is when his line of duty takes him among refugees, those weary, shuffling, hopeless columns, chiefly women, children and the aged, carrying or pushing-pulling pram, wheelbarrow, farm cart, piled high with their world and often perched on top – granny. If his unit is rushing forward, pressing these weary souls

40 aside so that the troops could get ahead and engage the enemy – he is sad, but feels he's giving them hope, but if his army is in retreat and they are in the press at the side of the road, the troops and guns rush past to take up another fighting position, he is sad but ashamed because he knows they think he is running away.

Just by was the church. Straw had been placed all round it and there were dark forms lying on it, My pal and I moved to the straw and were about to settle when we noticed two young women. With a mumbled apology, we were moving away when a voice said in good English, "Don't go, please." We squatted down, and I saw that one of the young women was nursing a whimpering baby. For something to say, I said, "Is your baby alright?" With a sad smile she said, "It's not my baby. I don't even know its mother, We

50 are tired and hungry." My pal and I emptied from our haversacks two tins of sardines and army biscuits. She sighed and said, "The baby needs milk." "Milk!" I swung my water-bottle round. I think even the baby was surprised. Quite soon, we fell in and marched away. The British government had lost a water-bottle, but a baby found a meal.

by Sergeant Richard Tobin, Hood Battalion, Royal Naval Division

Source 4 | Extract from **Tickling the English**

Dara O Briain is an Irish stand-up comedian and a television presenter. In *Tickling the English* he describes the places he has visited on tour in England and the audiences who have attended his gigs. In the introduction to this book he tells us that he will start by naming the venue and the people he spoke to.

Sheffield City Hall

George – who rolls steel
1 T-shirt designer
1 plumber
1 accountant
1 IT contractor

And so the gigs roll along happily, keeping my confidence high for the big DVD show at the weekend. Next up is a trip to Yorkshire, usually home to the most talkative people
10 in the country. Gigs in the past in Leeds, Selby, Bridlington, Halifax and Huddersfield have all been uniformly wonderful. Similarly, Sheffield is the home to one of the best comedy clubs in the country, The Last Laugh, a famously sweaty gig in the back room of the Lescar pub. You'd do a forty-minute set, and come off drenched and have to change in the kitchen as the punters wandered past the door. For some reason, I can still see the giant tubs of margarine, as I tried to look casual while conducting a post-mortem, shirtless and glistening, with show host Toby Foster.

20 This trip, I am doing my show at the City Hall, which is by no stretch of the imagination a sweaty room in the back of a pub. However, ten minutes into the show, and I am drenched again. But now it is with a cold, cold sweat. The kind you get when you realize that there are 1,950 people in the room and it just isn't working.

Let's see how this happened. I ran out to applause, mentioned a few of the other nights on the tour, hit them with the schtick about how much I was looking forward to chatting to them tonight and then said, 'Right, who's here?' and leaned
30 in toward the front row. And, instinctively, 1,950 people seemed to back away.

Have you ever made a room clench? That's what it felt like.

They puckered up. They curled into a ball. They went foetal. It was like doing a show to an alarmed hedgehog.

I managed to frighten a room full of people so badly, their natural defence mechanisms kicked in and they made a smaller target of themselves.

From the very start it was all one-word answers and nods. They were giving me absolutely nothing to work with, and all 40 the fluid that would normally be lubricating my mouth began to drench my shirt instead.

Dying onstage is a bizarre piece of evolutionary biology. Why exactly would we have developed a response to fear that dries the mouth and thickens the tongue just when we need them most? What caveman antics required this most specific of fight-or-flight responses?

If you've never gone through it, 50 these are the stages:

Firstly, panic. An internal panic when Plan A gets nothing, and a quick root around to find a Plan B. Secondly, a viscosity of the brain, When Plan B fails, it takes markedly longer to find Plan C. Sometimes you end up doing Plan A again. This is not good. It never works better the second time. The mouth 60 begins to dry now, and you suddenly become very aware of how bad this looks. Normally, on stage, you're not self-conscious at all. You're too busy doing the job even to consider how ridiculous it looks. When the laughs stop, there is a very sudden realization that you might look very foolish indeed in front of these people. This is the fight-or-flight moment. Do you politely exit, with some good grace and dignity, 70 or do you plough on and hope that something, anything, in your sorry script will gain some purchase with the crowd and turn this around?

The answer, hard-earned, is of course C: you stop what you're doing, tell the audience how shit it's going and blame them. You've done this before, it always works. The only difference is them and, frankly, you're a little disappointed. You've made the effort to come here and they haven't brought their A-game. You'll got through with this, but expect better, starting with the next joke.

80 Then you go back and do Plan A again.

This night in Sheffield wasn't quite death though, I had still a show I could do, I still had at least ninety minutes of tested material that I had no difficulty getting out, and that the crowd were enjoying, I just couldn't get them to engage in any one-to-ones. All the bonus, all the gravy of the off-the-cuff, all the ad-libbing to sprinkle on top of the show, all gone.

I walked off at half-time, and Damon was already there, going, 'I know, I know… Remember, though, you've not played the City Hall before. Maybe they just weren't expecting it to be
90 so… interactive.'

After the show, I was sitting, still a little shell-shocked, at the stage door, when a cheery punter passed by. 'That was great!' he said, and was genuinely surprised when I almost grabbed him by the collar.

'How the f*** was that great? You all said nothing to me! I couldn't get a word out of you!'

'Well, we didn't come to hear us. We came to hear you. That's what we're like in Sheffield, Bands get really thrown as well when we don't sing along. We come to hear them sing the
100 songs though.'

That's what they're like in Sheffield. They won't make cream with you, but they love the cake.

by Dara O Briain

Source 5 | Extract from **I Have Lived a Thousand Years**

In this extract from her memoir, written some 50 years later, the writer recalls how at the age of 13 years old, she and her mother were introduced to the cruelty and deprivation of one of Germany's most feared concentration camps.

The huge metal letters loom high and dark about the gothic gate like a sinister crown. WORK SETS YOU FREE. What does that mean? Could Mummy have been right? Could it be that we would work and be treated like human beings? Given food and proper lodgings? But free? What do they mean by that? Would they give us even freedom if we worked?

The immense portals of the gate open and we march through into an enclosure with tall wire fences. Very tall plain wire fences flanked on both sides by a lower fence of barbed wire.

It is rapidly growing lighter. And colder. Much colder. The eerie light of the
10 watchtowers is growing dimmer. When would we get our things? I need my coat. We keep marching. On and on. Past rows of barracks, long flat buildings on both sides of the pebble-strewn road lined with barbed wire. It is a road without an end. It stretches into the fog. And we keep marching.

Motorcycles roar past. SS officers. Dogs. Incessant barking. *'Marschieren. Marschieren! Los. Los!'*

We keep marching. On and on. It is bitter cold.

Clusters of people linger on both sides of the road, beyond the fence. Are they men or women? Shorn heads. Grey dresses. They run to the fence and stare. Blank stares. The blank stares of the insane. They have the appearance of the mentally ill. Impersonal.
20 This is probably an asylum for the mentally ill. Poor souls.

The road ends. Our silent, rapid, haunted march ends at the entrance of a grey, flat building. In fives we are ordered to file through the entrance. Inside, a long narrow room, very low ceiling. Inside, shocking noises. Shouts, screams. Loud unintelligible screams.

'Ruhe!' Quiet!

A tall husky blonde in SS uniform shouts, *'Ruuhee! Wer versteht Deutsch? Deutsch! Wer versteht Deutsch, 'raustreten!'* Who understands German? Step forward!

I step forward. I understand German. A few other girls also step forward. They probably also understand German.

'Tell them,' the big SS woman roars. She tosses a chair towards me. 'Stand on this and
30 tell them to keep quiet at once. I want quiet this minute. Next minute they will be shot!'

I attempt to shout above the din. And other interpreters, they too shout as loudly as they can. The low ceiling compresses the sound. The noise is like a roaring tidal wave hurling back and forth. Stunning us senseless.

'RUHE!' The buxom SS woman leans forward and cracks her whip into the crowd. As if on cue, the SS soldiers lining the walls step forward and begin cracking their whips, snapping into faces. A sharp pain slashes my left cheekbone. I feel a firm welt rise across my face. Why? I am the interpreter. Quickly, I step down and melt into the crowd. Perhaps it is safer there.

Within seconds it becomes quiet.

40 *'Auskleiden! Alles herunter!'* Everyone undress! Everything off! *'Los!'*

The room is swarming with SS men. Get undressed? Right here? In front of the men? No one moves.

'Didn't you hear? Take off your clothes. All your clothes!'

I feel the slap of the whip on my shoulders and meet a young SS soldier's glaring eyes. 'Hurry! Strip fast. You'll be shot. In five minutes anyone with clothes on will be shot!'

I look at Mummy. She nods. 'Let's get undressed.' I stare directly ahead as I take off my clothes. I am afraid, By not looking at anyone I hope no one will see me. I have never seen my mother in the nude. How awful it must be for her.

[...]

It is chilly and frightening. Clothes lie in mounds on the cement floor. We are herded, 50 over a thousand shivering, humiliated, nude bodies, into the next hall, even chillier, darker. Even barer and more foreboding.

'Los! Schneller, blöde Lumpen!' Move. Faster, idiotic whores.

We are lined up, and several young women in grey dresses start shaving our hair – on our heads, under our arms and in the pubic area. My long, thick plaits remain attached while the shaving machine shears my scalp. The pain of the heavy plait tugging mercilessly at the yet unshaven roots brings tears to my eyes. I whisper a silent prayer for the shaving to be done quickly. For this unexpected torture to be over soon.

[...]

The shaving of hair has a startling effect. The absence of hair transforms individual women into like bodies. Indistinguishable. Age melts away. Other personal differences 60 melt away. Facial expressions disappear. In their place, a blank senseless stare emerges on the thousand faces of one naked, unappealing body. In a matter of minutes even the physical aspect of our numbers seems reduced – there is less of a substance to our dimensions. We become a monolithic mass. Inconsequential.

The shaving of hair has another curious effect. A burden is lifted. The burden of individuality. The burden of associations. Of identity. The burden of the recent past. Girls who had continually wept since the separation from parents, sisters and

brothers, now keep giggling at their friends' strange appearances – shorn heads, nude bodies, faceless faces. Some shriek with laughter. Others begin calling out names of friends to see if they can recognize them now. When response comes from completely
70 transformed bodies, recognition is loud, hysterical. Embraces are wild, noisy. Disbelief is shrieked, screamed, gesticulated. Some girls bury their faces in their palms and roll on the ground, howling.

'*Was ist los?*' What's the matter? A few cracks of the SS whip, and order is restored.

I look for Mummy. I find her easily. The hair cropping has not changed her for me. I have been used to seeing her in her kerchiefs, every bit of hair carefully tucked away. Avoiding a glance at her body, I marvel at the beauty of her face. With all accessories gone, her perfect features are even more striking. Her high forehead, large blue eyes, classic nose, shapely lips, and elegant cheekbones are more evident than ever.

She does not recognize me as I stand before her. Then, a sudden smile of recognition:
80 'Elli! It's you! You look just like your Bubi. Strange, I've never seen the resemblance before. What a boyish face! They cut off your beautiful plaits...'

'It's nothing. Hair can grow.'

'With God's help.'

We are herded *en masse* into the next hall. I shriek with sudden shock as a cold torrent of water gushes unexpectedly from openings in the ceiling. The mass of wet, nude bodies crushes about me in a mad, splattering wave. In a few minutes it is over and I am carried along in the midst of the wet mass to another hall. Grey, sack-like dresses are shoved at us and we are ordered with shouts of '*Los, blöde Schweine*' to pull them over wet, shivering bodies. The epithet '*blöde Lumpen*', idiotic whores, is now
90 downgraded to '*blöde Schweine*', idiotic swine. More despicable. And it is upgraded only occasionally to '*blöde Hunde*', idiotic dogs. Easier to handle, Everyone has to pick a pair of shoes from an enormous shoe pile. '*Los! Los!*' Take a pair, Size makes no difference.

As we emerge from the other end of the building and line up quickly in rows of five, shivering wet in shapeless grey sacks, with heads cleanshaven, the idea strikes me. The strange creatures we saw as we entered the camp, the shaven, grey-cloaked bunch who ran to the barbed-wire fence to stare at us, we are them! We look exactly like them. Same bodies, same dresses, same blank stares. They, too, must have arrived from home recently. They, too, were ripe women and young girls, bewildered and bruised. They, too, longed for dignity and compassion. And they, too, were transformed into figures of
100 contempt instead.

The *Zählappell* lasts almost three hours. This word, meaning roll call, becomes the dread and the lifestyle of Auschwiz. Twice daily we are lined up in fives to be counted. At 3 a.m. we would line up with lightning speed, and then stand stiffly and silently for three or four hours until the official SS staff shows up to count our heads. The SS officer taps the heads of the first line and counts in multiples of five. The actual count

is accomplished in a few minutes. The stiff, silent wait on the evening *Zählappell* lasts from five to nine. The line-up has to be mustered in seconds in order to stand for hours, waiting.

It is inconceivable to me that the mad rush inside would culminate in an
110 interminable wait outside. Why are our wet, traumatized bodies, wearing only a single cotton cloak, hurled out into the cold for an endless, senseless wait?

Finally, a smartly stepping, brisk German military staff member appears. With the tap of an authoritarian stick on the shaven head of the first girl in every row of five, we are initiated into the camp. We have become members of an exclusive club. Inmates of Auschwitz.

by Livia Bitton-Jackson

Source 6 | Extract from **Samuel Pepys: The Unequalled Self**

In this extract from her biography of the famous diarist Samuel Pepys (1633–1703), Claire Tomalin examines his character and personality, as shown through one of his diary entries.

At seven o'clock on a January morning, as the sky over London was growing light, a row broke out in a bedroom between a husband and wife. They had been to the theatre the night before, and afterwards had to wait nearly an hour for a cab. When they finally reached home, rather than going to bed, he insisted on returning to his office – it was across the yard – to finish some work. So although he was usually the first awake and out of bed on a weekday, on this particular day he was sleeping in; or at least he was hoping to.
10 Instead he was awoken by an angry and tearful wife.

Still lying in bed and only half awake, he began to take in what she was saying. At first it was a complicated account about a maid they had recently dismissed who was spreading stories, accusing her of giving away his money to her family. He had no intention of arguing about this and tactfully calmed her until they appeared to be friends again; but at that point her real grievance appeared, and turned out to be something different and worse. What was really upsetting her, she said, was that she was lonely. She suffered so much from loneliness
20 that she had written him a letter expressing her unhappiness, she reminded him, and handed it to him two months ago. But he had refused to read it and burnt it without even reading her carefully chosen words.

Now she told him she had kept a copy – it was something she must have learnt from his meticulous office habits – and she called her maid Jane into the bedroom, gave her the keys of her trunk and told her to fetch the bundle of papers she kept locked inside. Jane, who knew both of them well and had witnessed many scenes, brought the papers and discreetly left
30 the room again. Elizabeth Pepys began to read the letter aloud to her husband. The scene is played out in front of us on the page of his Diary: it is Friday, 9 January 1663.

His wife's letter impressed Pepys so much he began to worry about its falling into anyone else's hands. It was

"picquant, and wrote in English and most of it true" – he specified English because French came as naturally to her – and it would reflect badly on him. He asked her to tear it up and when she did not respond, he ordered her to do so. She refused. He snatched it from her along with the whole bundle
40 of her private papers; then he got out of bed in his nightshirt and stuffed them all into the large pockets of his breeches, which were lying by the bed. He had to struggle into his breeches and put on his stockings and gown, defending

himself from her attempts to retrieve her property. When he was half dressed, he started pulling the papers out again
50 and tearing them up one by one, while she cried and begged to have them back. By now she was more distressed than she had been at the start of their talk, and he was in a rage. He let his anger flare up so
60 fiercely that when he came to his own love letters he began to tear them up too. Then he tore up the copy of the will he had written and given her, in which he had left her all he had.

Yet all the time a
70 corner of himself was calm enough to notice and set aside certain papers. There was a bond and their marriage licence: money and the law must be respected. He also spared the first letter he had ever sent her; and, when he felt he had gone far enough to make

his point, he took all the papers, the ones he had torn and the ones he had spared, into his own room and considered whether he should burn them. He put aside the pieces of his will and of her letter to him that had started the trouble, and all the papers he had left intact. Everything else went on 80 the fire. After that he finished dressing and departed for the office, "troubled in mind".

We know all this because he described it himself. In writing it down, he detached himself from the self who acted out the scene. He watched himself, just as he watched Elizabeth, or Jane; just as he had watched the players and the audience in the theatre the night before. His conflicting emotions – indignation and anger, pity for her and acknowledgement that she was justified in what she had done – make this as absorbing as a scene in a play or novel. It is life, but as he 90 writes it down it becomes art; and it is the art of a diarist of genius, one who does not choose to give himself the *beau rôle*. Later in his career Pepys sometimes stood greatly on his own dignity, but here in the pages of his own Diary he assumes none of the gravitas we should all like to claim for ourselves in a bedroom row. He struggles into his breeches, he behaves unjustly and cruelly, he offers no justification of any kind for his behaviour except his anger and fear of being blamed. This is what he had seen and what he had felt, transmuted into words.

The quarrel was made up in the evening, but the morning scene was a painful landmark in the marriage. To both husband and wife the written word was of great importance. Both were readers, and the destruction of the written evidence of their love and its history was a symbolic act. The marriage, which had never been calm, became increasingly stormy after this.

by Claire Tomalin

Source 7 | The Sunday Morning Markets

Written in the mid-nineteenth century, this richly detailed description of a Sunday market reveals much about both the place and the people who frequented it.

Nearly every poor man's market does its Sunday trade. For a few hours on the Sabbath morning, the noise, bustle, and scramble of the Saturday night are repeated, and but for this opportunity many a poor family would pass a dinnerless Sunday. The system of paying the mechanic late on the Saturday night – and more particularly of paying a man his wages in a public-house – when he is tired with his day's work lures him to the tavern, and there the hours fly quickly enough beside the warm tap-room fire, so that by the time the
10 wife comes for her husband's wages, she finds a large portion of them gone in drink, and the streets half cleared, so that the Sunday market is the only chance of getting the Sunday's dinner.

Of all these Sunday-morning markets, the Brill, perhaps, furnishes the busiest scene; so that it may be taken as a type of the whole.

The streets in the neighbourhood are quiet and empty. The shops are closed with their different-coloured shutters, and the people round about are dressed in the shiny cloth of the
20 holiday suit. There are no "cabs," and but few omnibuses to disturb the rest, and men walk in the road as safely as on the footpath.

As you enter the Brill the market sounds are scarcely heard. But at each step the low hum grows gradually into the noisy shouting, until at last the different cries become distinct, and the hubbub, din, and confusion of a thousand voices bellowing at once again fill the air. The road and footpath are crowded, as on the over-night; the men are standing in groups, smoking and talking; whilst the women run to and fro, some with the
30 white round turnips showing out of their filled aprons, others with cabbages under their arms, and a piece of red meat dangling from their hands. Only a few of the shops are closed, but the butcher's and the coal-shed are filled with customers, and from the door of the shut-up baker's, the women come streaming forth with bags of flour in their hands, while men sally from the halfpenny barber's smoothing their clean-shaved chins. Walnuts, blacking, apples, onions, braces, combs, turnips, herrings, pens, and corn-plaster, are all bellowed out at the same time. Labourers and mechanics, still unshorn and
40 undressed, hang about with their hands in their pockets, some with their pet terriers under their arms. The pavement is green

with the refuse leaves of vegetables, and round a cabbage-barrow the women stand turning over the bunches, as the man shouts, "Where you like, only a penny." Boys are running home with the breakfast herring held in a piece of paper, and the side-pocket of the apple-man's stuff coat hangs down with the weight of the halfpence stored within it.

Presently the tolling of the neighbouring church bells breaks forth. Then the bustle doubles itself, the cries grow
50 louder, the confusion greater. Women run about and push their way through the throng, scolding the saunterers, for in half an hour the market will close. In a little time the butcher puts up his shutters, and leaves the door still open; the policemen in their clean gloves come round and drive the street-sellers before them, and as the clock strikes eleven the market finishes, and the Sunday's rest begins.

by Henry Mayhew

53

Source 8 | Taking a Picture

In this account we discover the lengths a determined photographer will go to in order to get a picture of a lifetime!

Leaving Lembogi, Kabechi and the old guide behind, I took the cameras and ran down the slope, crossed the bog and climbed up the far side, Mohammed was to follow at a short distance, on account of the clatter of his boots on the rocks. I drew to within forty yards of the rhino, yet they still looked like a couple of grey boulders as they browsed off an isolated patch of sere grass.

The wind had risen to a tearing gale, and nosing straight into it I approached the rhino somewhat downhill. There
10 was no chance of this steady blow jumping round to betray me, and it was strong enough to carry away any sound of my footsteps. Precaution was therefore unnecessary and I walked boldly up to them. Just how close I was, it is hard to say; but I noted subconsciously that the eye of the one nearest me was not dark brown as I imagined it, but the colour of sherry.

And the experience has left me in some doubt whether a rhino has such poor eye sight as is commonly believed. Perhaps they heard the clicking of the cinema camera. This may have given the nearer one my direction, and then my coat or the brim of my
20 hat flapping in the wind possibly caught his eye. At any rate, his ears pricked up, his champing jaws were held in suspense and that little pale eye was very definitely focused straight upon me.

He lifted his head, trying to catch the wind. It told him nothing, but he now came deliberately towards me, nose to the ground and horn foremost. I pressed the button and tried to keep a steady hand. This was not easy; for a rhino seen through the finder of a small cinema camera looks remote, and it is only when you take the camera down to make sure, that you are horribly startled to see how near he really is. In the finder I saw
30 his tail go up, and knew that he was on the point of charging. Though it was the impression of a fraction of a second, it was unforgettable. He was standing squarely upon a flat boulder that raised him like a pedestal, and he seemed to tower up rugged and clear-cut as a monument against the flying clouds.

Such a chance could never possibly occur again, and the magnificence of that picture for the moment blinded me to all else. I read the danger signal, yet in a kind of trance of excitement I still held the camera against my forehead. Then Mohammed fired a shot over the rhino's head to scare him,
40 and I turned and fled for my life.

The rhino was only momentarily taken aback. Before I had time to skip out of his sight he had made up his mind to charge me. The angry thunder of his snort, mingled with a screech like an engine blowing off steam, lent me wings. When I dared to throw a backward glance I saw that both rhino were bearing down upon me with frightening speed. The boys had had a start of me, and as I raced after them across the vistas of stone without a blade of cover anywhere, conviction swept over me that this time the game was up.

50   Though I ran and ran as I had never run in my life before, and my heart pounded in my ears and my lungs stiffened with the pain of drawing breath, time went suddenly into slow motion. Each step was weighted with lead; I wanted to fly over the ground and, as in some horrid nightmare, I felt as though I were scarcely moving.

The rhino were swiftly gaining upon me; their furious snorts overtook me on the wings of the gale. The boys, on the other hand, had disappeared as though the earth had swallowed them. I made one more desperate spurt and then, 60 as I realised the utter futility of it, a fold in the hillside opened to receive me also. I tumbled headlong down a little cliff and landed on a ledge of heather.

The rhino would never face this drop even if they looked over and saw me. I glanced up apprehensively, but there was no sign of them.

In this sheltered place there was not a sound, and even the wind had dropped, With thankful heart I stretched myself face 70 downward on the heather, and panted as though I could never get a complete lungful of air again, while waves of crimson and orange rushed and throbbed before my eyes.

The boys climbed up to me (they had landed farther down) and seeing Mohamed's expression of disapproval I quickly put my word in first.

"That," said I, "is the best picture I have ever taken!"

by Vivienne de Watteville

Source 9 | Getups

Do 'clothes make the man'? In this short extract, the renowned African American writer Maya Angelou gives us an insight into her own wardrobe and her views on the clothes worn by others.

I was a twenty-one-year-old single parent with my son in kindergarten. Two jobs allowed me an apartment, food, and child care payment. Little money was left over for clothes, but I kept us nicely dressed in discoveries bought at the Salvation Army and other secondhand shops. Loving colors, I bought for myself beautiful reds and oranges, and greens and pinks, and teal and turquoise. I chose azure dresses and blouses and sweaters. And quite often I wore them in mixtures which brought surprise, to say the least, to the eyes of people

10 who could not avoid noticing me. In fact, I concocted what southern black women used to call "getups."

Because I was very keen that my son not feel that he was neglected or different, I went frequently to his school. Sometimes between my jobs I would just go and stand outside the fenced play area. And he would, I am happy to say, always come and acknowledge me in the colourful regalia. I always wore beads. Lots of beads. The cheaper they were, the more I got, and sometimes I wore head wraps.

When my son was six and I twenty-two, he told me quite
20 solemnly that he had to talk to me. We both sat down at the kitchen table, and he asked with an old man's eyes and a young boy's voice, "Mother, do you have any sweaters that match?" I was puzzled at first. I said, "No," and then I understood he was talking about the pullover and cardigan sets which were popular with white women. And I said, "No, I don't," maybe a little huffily. And he said, "Oh, I wish you did. So that you could wear them to school when you come to see me."

I was tickled, but I am glad I didn't laugh because he continued, "Mother, could you please only come to school
30 when they call you?" Then I realized that my attire, which delighted my heart and certainly activated my creativity, was an embarrassment to him.

When people are young, they desperately need to conform, and no one can embarrass a young person in public so much as an adult to whom he or she is related. Any outré action or wearing of "getups" can make a young person burn with self-consciousness.

I learned to be a little more discreet to avoid causing him displeasure. As he grew older and more confident, I gradually
40 returned to what friends thought of as my eccentric way of dressing. I was happier when I chose and created my own

fashion. I have lived in this body all my life and know it much better than any fashion designer. I think I know what looks good on me, and I certainly know what feels good on me.

I appreciate the creativity which is employed in the design of fabric and the design of clothes, and when something does fit my body and personality, I rush to it, buy it quickly, and wear it frequently. But I must not lie to myself for fashion's sake. I am only willing to purchase the item which becomes me and to

50 wear that which enhances my image of myself to myself.

If I am comfortable inside my skin, I have the ability to make other people comfortable inside their skins although their feelings are not my primary reason for making my fashion choice. If I feel good inside my skin and clothes, I am thus free to allow my body its sway, its natural grace, its natural gesture. Then I am so comfortable that whatever I wear looks good on me even to the external fashion arbiters.

Dress is important to mention because many people are imprisoned by powerful dictates on what is right and proper

60 to wear. Those decisions made by others and sometimes at their convenience are not truly meant to make life better or finer or more graceful or more gracious. Many times they stem from greed, insensitivity, and the need for control.

I have been in company, not long to be sure, but in company where a purveyor of taste will look at a woman or man who enters a room and will say with a sneer, "That was last year's jacket." As hastily as possible, I leave that company, but not before I record the snide attitude which has nothing to do with the beauty or effectiveness of the garment, but rather gives the

70 speaker a moment's sense of superiority at, of course, someone else's expense.

Seek the fashion which truly fits and befits you. You will always be in fashion if you are true to yourself, and only if you are true to yourself. You might, of course, rightly wear that style which is emblazoned on the pages of the fashion magazines of the day, or you might not.

The statement "Clothes make the man" should be looked at, re-examined, and in fact re-evaluated. Clothes can make the man or woman look silly and foppish and foolish. Try rather to

80 be so much yourself that the clothes you choose increase your naturalness and grace.

by Maya Angelou

Source 10 | Extract from My Father's Fortune

In this short extract, the writer shows that love at first sight can happen.

So there she was, the girl Bert Crouchman was after. Vi. Violet Alice Lawson. My mother.

I gaze at the old photographs of her in my album and see something of what my father saw when he walked into that party with Bert. A heart-shaped face and wide, wide eyes. Piled brown hair and plaits down to her waist. In one of the photographs she looks straight out at me as perhaps she did at him that evening.

Tom looked at her, and she looked at him – and that was it. He was eighteen, and for him those few short years of girls, plural, were suddenly over. She was still only fourteen, and boys, plural, can hardly have begun. Their lives were settled for the next
10 thirty years.

It was her younger sister, my Auntie Phyllis, who told me about how they met.[...] 'Tommy went straight up to Vi,' and said "I'm Tom – I suppose you're Vi!" And from then on, nobody else got a look-in.' 'Poor Bert,' said Phyllis, 'must have wished he'd never mentioned that party to Tom'. What happened to Bert thereafter she didn't record. He had dropped away from the story like the launch stage of a space rocket.

Fourteen-year-old Vi and eighteen-year-old Tom – or Tommy, as he now became to Vi and all her side of the family. From Phyllis's account of the way he introduced himself he sounds as if he was at his most self-assured that evening, as much the cocky young man of the world as he looks in his photographs. I expect he gave her one of his
20 irresistible smiles. Soon, I imagine, he was demonstrating his double-jointedness to her – bending his fingers backwards against the table in a sickeningly unnatural reverse curve, and pushing back the thumb on his right hand until it seemed ready to snap off. Then showing her his other special attraction, the thumb on his left hand, that couldn't be bent at all, because there was no joint in it to be even single; his brother George, the compositor, had showed him round the printing works when he was a boy, and allowed him to put his hand in a press.

I suppose she looked up at him with those wide eyes, and that hopelessly appealing plangency in her heart-shaped face. Fourteen, going on fifteen, confronting eighteen, going on twenty-five. She saw the way he was looking at her – he saw the way she was
30 looking at him – and by the time they had finished looking the story of their lives was half-written.

by Michael Frayn

Source 11 | The New Boy

Attending school in Scotland presents many challenges for the writer; not least the unwanted attention his unusual accent draws from the other boys.

I travelled every morning with Uncle Duff, [...] he to his office in St Vincent Street, me to George Square and the long haul up the cobbled stone street to The School. Standing isolated in the centre of a vast asphalted playground, surrounded by high iron spikes, its red sandstone blocks rotting in the filth from the city, it resembled a cross between a lunatic asylum and a cotton mill. Faceless windows gazed blankly over the streets below. Electric lights gleamed dully even on the clearest days. A smell of chalk and concrete dust,
10 of sulphur and soot.

Green glazed tiles, ochre distemper, red varnished wood. Cold, unloving, unloved. A Technical School for Technical People. What on earth was I doing here? I who could only just about read and write? Chosen by Uncle Duff for a "good solid back-ground under a progressive teaching staff", it was thoughtfully accepted by my parents as the Final Desperate Measure to try and force some learning into my addled head. They had made a swift tour of the place, dragging me in stupefied horror behind them, had shaken hands in a cramped
20 Victorian headmaster's Study and departed with relief for the South leaving me to sort out the road leading to "The Times".

It was only a matter of days before I knew, for certain, that I was in the very worst place for my sort of complaint. I had the technical brain of a newt.[...] I never knew how many apples a farmer had left in his basket if he gave his wife two-thirds. Or how much water slipped away in an hour if the bath-plug was released and the tap dripped at the rate of fifty drops per minute. What the Hell! I was lost. Notebooks were virginal white. Pencils unblunted. Rubbers un-rubbed.
30 Surrounded by a class of thirty I started to observe them in preference to the impossible messages on the blackboards.

Raw-boned hulks most of them seemed. Red hair and freckles; fair hair and pigs' eyes; white faces and acne. Stooped grey-flannel backs, prematurely humped, arms like gorillas stretched out along their desks: booted feet twitching for a football. Or anything to kick.

No vivid Trevor Ropes, no fat kind Foots, no bespectacled Jones G.C.'s here. These were tough, Irish-Scots, one parent away from the Pits, four years or less from the Barricades.
40 Foreigners. And what made things harder was that I couldn't understand a word they said, nor could they understand me.

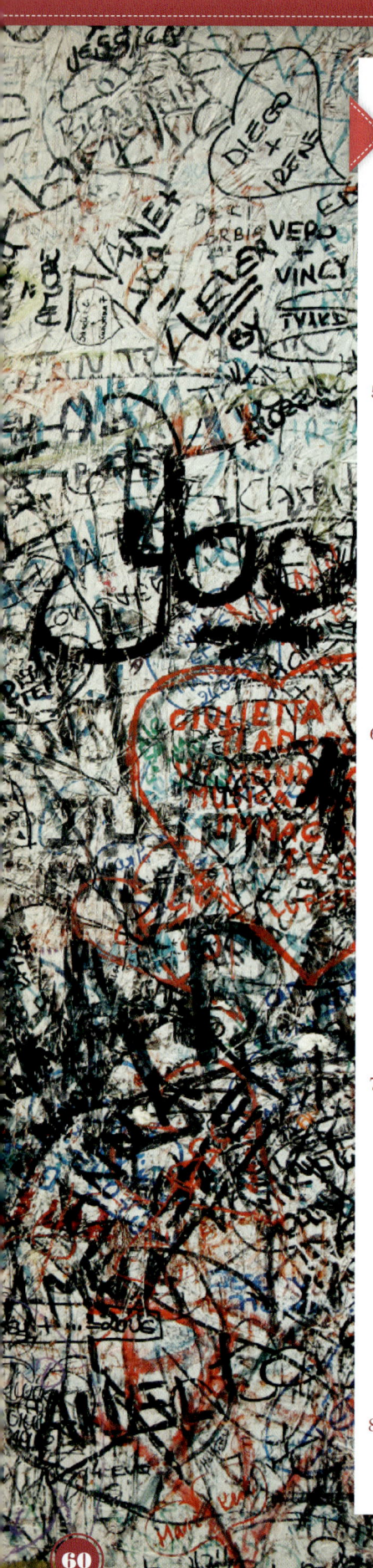

A gulf had started from the very first day with the barrier of our common tongue. I was the odd man out, the Sassenach, posh, weedy, incomprehensible, alien. But I knew that because I was New, this slit-eyed raw-boned herd of bullocks was biding its time until the terror which was growing steadily within me should start to leak away, like blood in a sea of sharks. And when they scented it, they would attack. This I knew.

50   My desk mate – we sat two to a bench like slaves in the galleys – was called Tom. He was dark, thin, pleasant looking with round tin glasses. He showed me where to hang my cap and coat, where my locker was, where the lavatories were, the class-rooms I would use, and where to eat our lunch if we didn't go home. Which neither of us did.

A long brick shed, it was pushed into a corner of the Yard almost as an afterthought. It had a tin roof and was euphemistically called the Tuck Shop. Banks of greasy wooden tables, benches on each side, a long counter at one end with tea and coffee urns and racks of soggy hot, or cold, meat pies,
60   sausages, cheese buns, bread and dripping and Mars Bars.

At the other end, two pin tables for the elder boys. We were not allowed to use them until we were sixteen, but everyone did anyway. In one corner a foul, stinking lavatory which was three walls with an open drain round the edges. Sluggish streams of gently steaming urine bubbled along this trough. Cigarette ends and gobs of spittle bobbed about like floats in a stream. On the walls above the slate slabs, against which we pissed, a whole holocaust of wild scribbles and obscenities, none of which I understood.

70   Tom used to guide me out of the Tuck Shop as often as the weather allowed and we sat, each with our bottle of Cola, a hot pie and an apple or an orange, on the low wall which ran round the dustbins watching a thousand games of football played with an old tennis ball or a rough block of wood. He talked away from time to time, and I tried to understand him, which made him laugh and he tried to understand me, which made me laugh too. [...] I liked him very much, and he became my mate.

One day when the weather was too wet to go out and
80   eat our lunch on the dustbin wall, some of the Herd started to make muffled, smothered, giggling jokes clearly about

me across the greasy tables. They were mostly the elder boys, and the younger ones were sniggering and squirming sycophantically at the jokes. Tom suddenly stiffened with alarm and mumbled something, but before he was able to say anything more, the Herd had started to move towards me in a slow, undulating wave. With one united lunge they grabbed me and dragged me struggling in nameless terror to the lavatory at the end of the room. I heard Tom shouting, but the 90 doors had swung closed and I was hustled into the cabin, up-ended into the lavatory pan, held firmly by my knees and legs, while someone, as if from a hundred miles down a tunnel, said: "Fuckin' posh twit. Talking so la-di-da need your wee mouth washin' out." Someone pulled the chain and I thought that I had drowned. Gasping and choking, vomiting like a dog on the wet slimy floor, I was told that until I learned to speak correctly this would happen again. Then they left me. I lay for an eternity, retching and gasping in a sea of filth and undigested meat pie. I thought that I would never be able to 100 breathe again. Tears and dribble coursed down my face from the coughing and choking and the retching.

Tom helped me to clean up as best I could in the boiler room under the school. [...] I stayed there hiccupping and heaving until the break bell clanged. Damp, creased and smelly I took my place in Class. No one said anything. They watched over the tops of their books or sideways from the edges of their faces. They were all quietly smiling. Through bleary eyes I looked back at them. And decided to learn to speak correctly.

110 For days I was in terror that I should catch some disease from my Lavatory Drowning. [...] I bought a bottle of disinfectant and, as secretly as I could, gargled and cleaned my mouth out until it was raw and blistered. No one knew what had happened, of course, and I had a difficult job sneaking into the house and changing my filthy clothes, but managed to convince them that I had been in a fight in the rain.

Uncle Duff was quite jovial at tea that evening.

"A fight already! Well I declare! they'll make a wee man of ye yet."

120 My aunt was no fool. She didn't say a word, just went on buttering her potato pancake, but I think she knew that it had been more than a fight.

For the first month or two I was bullied constantly. Being skinny, having the wrong accent, although I was doing my damnedest to correct that daily, and never joining in the break time football made me conspicuous. And I was accordingly treated as such, for that is really what they thought I was. Different, weak, a cissie, to be got rid of. Tom was a help, but I felt that I couldn't shelter behind him all the time, and in any

130 case, he wasn't always with me. He had his learning to do and was frequently taking a different Class to me.

Sitting one day on the wall of the Yard (there were no benches) I got clouted on the shin by a whirling block of wood being used as a football. I yelled out in pain and fell off the wall. I was suddenly engulfed in a swirling, kicking mass of roaring footballers who dragged me across the asphalt in the direction of the lavatory. Terror loaned me desperate strength. I fought and clawed and bit and kicked and suddenly found that the crowd had pulled away and I was struggling with one

140 sole boy, older than me, taller, and stronger. His name, I think, was Bell. I don't know what happened, or how I did it, but as he swung me away from him with one arm to punch me in the face, I swung at him and hit him with all the force I could muster in the eye. He gave a great cry and fell to the ground, his face covered with his hands. I fell on top of him and went on bashing and thumping at him, but his cries grew louder and louder, and his hands flew from his face and flailed the air about his head. I saw that he now only had one eye. The other had apparently gone.

150 We were dragged to our feet, I stiff with terror at the pulp-face before me; he barking in a loud hoarse voice, blood streaming down his face.

Whitefaced, they half carried, half led, him across to the school. I stood alone in the middle of the yard. No one moved or spoke. They stood and watched me. Somebody pointed silently to a water tap over by the wall, and they watched in little groups as I bathed my face and washed off the blood which seemed to be more his than mine. When I straightened up they had gone. I was never bullied again. Avoided for a

160 time, but never bullied.

by Dirk Bogarde

Source 12 |
Extract from
Mawson's Will

In this extract the
writer focuses
on one of many
testing moments for
Douglas Mawson
who, against the
odds, survived
a disastrous
expedition to the
Antarctic in 1912.

On the morning of January 17, ignoring the falling snow and the virtual white-out, he tramped on a course 20 degrees west of north, grimly set on covering at least another five miles. A plain of ice and snow, on the spine of the Mertz Glacier, rose in front of him. He could feel the ascent, but could not see it. The pressure underfoot was on his toes as, bent almost double, he carted his burden into the morning.

He toiled a long, rising slope, heavily covered with snow. The sun was hidden, but its light and warmth filtered through 10 the low cloud. He took off his waterproof jacket for easier movement and, along with his gloves, tied it on the back of the sledge. He strained his eyes to find the safest path in the horrible, deceptive glare. Several times he stopped short of open-mouthed crevasses; twice he actually scraped past gaping cracks he had not seen. He then came on smooth snow, and the sledge was running well when without any sign – he went through to his thighs. He clambered out with some effort and resumed his climb up the slope. Peering out from under his goggles, he made out the line of the crevasse on the edge of 20 which he had just fallen through. It went to the south beyond vision; he turned to the north, and, 50 yards farther on, all trace had vanished into a field of flat, clear snow that offered him a path back to his westering course.

In the next instant, he felt himself falling, his stomach a plummeting lead weight. Then the rope yanked viciously, cutting the harness into his body, bringing a sea of bright-coloured pain. He was suspended over a black, bottomless chasm. Now he could feel the sledge, pulled by his weight, sliding across the snow toward the edge of this icy pit – nearer 30 and nearer. In seconds the bulk of the sledge would rush over the broken snow bridge and then he would fall into the abyss. The thought flashed to his mind: "So—this is the end!"

The movement stopped. Against some unseen ridge or roll of snow-drift, the sledge halted; and now he swung fourteen feet down between sheer walls of steely-blue ice, six feet apart.

Slowly he spun in the crevasse, drooping with despair, at the end of the rope. Above, the lowering sky was a narrow band of light; below him were unseen black depths. Cautiously lifting his arms, he could just touch the crevasse walls.

40 Smooth and cold, they offered no fingerhold. Overhead the light showed the line of the rope cutting deep into the broken snow bridge, and he was fearful that sudden movement could again start the sledge sliding toward the edge. He held his position; the sledge did not move when he swung his legs in a wide arc. Gratitude filled his heart: "God has given me another chance…" A small, slim chance. Yet, how could he haul his weight directly upward on 14 feet of rope with his bare hands, his clothing full of snow, his body weak from starvation? Despairing, he turned his mind to the sledge propped in the
50 snow above.

How much did it weigh? Would it hold his weight if he tried to climb? He pictured his possessions on the abbreviated sledge, and instantly he saw the bag of food stacked on the mid-platform, and in the fear that clouded his brain he knew that he must make every effort to reach the bag.

The thought of wasted food galvanized him to action, and he was reaching a long skinny arm above his head, closing his bare fingers around the first knot in the rope. Shutting his mind against pain and stress, he lunged upward with his other hand and pulled his chin level. Again the reach—and he was six feet nearer the ledge; once more, and then again, holding the rope between his knees, feeling for the knots with his feet now—and he was level with the broken snow bridge. The treacherous, compacted snow was crumbling. Several times he tried to crawl to safety, and he was halfway to solid ice when the whole ledge fragmented under him. Again he crashed to the full length of the rope.

Once more the sledge held its grip in the snow. Once more he dangled, limp, drained, suspended in the chill half light. His hands were bleeding, all the skin of his palms had gone, his fingertips were black, and his body was freezing fast from the snow clogging his clothing, the deep cold of the ice walls shutting him in. He asked—why just hang here waiting for a frozen death? Why not end it all quickly, be done with the pain, the suffering, the struggles. Later he would write: "It was a moment of rare temptation. To quit small things for great, to pass from petty exploration of this world to vaster worlds beyond…" At the back of his belt was the razor-sharp sheath-knife. A good slash, a moment or two of breathless rush, and then, final peace—and no one would ever know how it ended, what had happened to him. He could see the sorrowing face of his beloved Paquita, the faces of his comrades—and he pictured again the food waiting on the surface […]—Buck up! Do your damndest and fight. Try again!

His strength was draining fast, he was growing deadly cold. Soon it would all be over and done with. But Providence still had him at the end of the rope that was a way back to the surface. By what he later called a "supreme effort," he scaled the rope, know after knot, and with a wild, flailing kick, thrust himself into the snow above the solid ice. He fell into a faint and lay unconscious, his face toward the sky, his hands bleeding into the snow.

by Lennard Bickel

Journalism

What is journalism?

Journalism is the communication of news and current events. Like non-fiction, its content is based on fact. Unlike much non-fiction, however, it is designed to have an immediate effect with the journalist writing for the reader of the following week, day or even hour.

Types of Journalism

There are many different types of texts which can be included under the heading of 'Journalism'. News reports are an obvious place to start. In these the journalist aim is to inform the reader of current events locally, nationally and internationally. They can include reports on disasters, wars, politics, business, sport and much more. Then there are feature stories. These can be about any subject; many are focused on lifestyle but there are others, which include tough investigative reporting on past events or important social issues. Feature stories tend to be longer than news reports and often rely heavily on the attitudes and opinions of the writer; language is used to inform, entertain and often persuade the reader.

Photographs are also a key feature of many types of journalism and can sometimes convey more in one image than a whole passage of text. People often respond strongly to visual images; many newspapers are bought for the striking heading and photograph, which first draws the readers' attention, rather than for the qualities of the articles which lie within.

Changing World

The world of journalism is changing rapidly. Where once people bought a daily newspaper or magazine, they now regularly read the news online, accessing it through laptops, smart phones and tablets. For the purpose of this Anthology, therefore, the term 'Journalism' has been used to incorporate anything that might appear in newspapers and magazines, either in print or online.

You will find a wide range of texts including a charity campaign, news items, feature stories, front pages and photographs. They are intended to give you an overview and insight into the vast range of material that is available for you to enjoy and explore on a daily basis.

Source 1 | Keep the flame alive

What is the real legacy of the Olympic Games? Sarah Crompton poses the question and comes up with some unexpected answers.

Keep the flame alive
The Olympic legacy and the new country we could be

If we can revive the spirit of common good that made the Games such a success in the straitened times ahead, their legacy will be complete

London 2012 has, at times, seemed like a throwback to an older, gentler Britain, where kindness and generosity were the order of the day. There may be towering fences and huge steel roadblocks surrounding the Olympic venues, but in and around those compounds a different spirit has been allowed to flourish.

Never before in this century have you seen so many people draped in the British flag. It has become the fashion accessory of the moment, thrown elegantly over shoulders, tied around jeans, worn as a jaunty plastic bowler, painted on cheeks and nails, vigorously waved.

That adoption of the flag is more than superficial. It is a symbol of the pride that people have felt as the athletes on the track, the sailors and rowers, the dancing horses and their riders, the cyclists, the fighters and swimmers, have struggled and shone for Team GB. In turn, that slightly clumsy ad man's phrase has come to feel like a truth: we are all in this together, a country united.

No wonder people's attention has turned to legacy, to keeping these feelings alive when the Games have gone, and the Olympic flame is just a fading photograph, not a real cauldron.

...

So when we try to draw lessons from the Games, instead of bandying words around, we should pause, think and recall the moments we have witnessed, creating a kind of manifesto of memories which will stand us in good stead in the bleak months ahead.

One of our first acts should be to acknowledge something we knew but had half forgotten – that we are actually quite good at this kind of thing. We can build a huge temporary city within our capital, welcome thousands of extra visitors, and make it work.

...

That efficiency looks back to the past, but should continue. The Games have allowed Britain, almost for the first time in memory, to celebrate its history while acknowledging its rich multicultural present, which is now leading the way into the future. We have seen a country at ease with its past, capable of sticking a ritzy beach volleyball court in the middle of Horse Guards Parade, or

Young athletes carry the torch to light the Olympic flame

its monarch in a sketch about a spy and a helicopter. But that narrative must also encompass the tolerance that welcomed Mo Farah when he arrived as a child from Somalia – and which has been rewarded with one of the best pictures of the Games, the sight of Britain's greatest distance runner wrapped in a flag, hugging his wife and child, applauded to the skies.

The exploits of our sportsmen and women, the memories they have conjured, have been inspiring in all sorts of ways. After this Olympics, nobody can claim that women's sports are second best. Every little girl who went to Wembley to see US v Japan, or caught a glimpse of the British women's team's valiant efforts on TV, will know once and for all that football doesn't belong to blokes; it belongs to them as well. There are girls' football leagues across Britain that should benefit.

As for Nicola Adams and her Irish counterpart, Katie Taylor, they have not only made redundant any arguments about the rightness of women boxing, they have also revealed their discipline in all its glory, as a sport of strength, speed and grace, not slugging in corners. Their legacy will be huge.

But the athletes have also offered a view of Britain as a complete society, North and South, rich and poor. On this team, the dressage gold-medal winner Charlotte Dujardin on her horse worth millions happily rubs shoulders with Louis Smith, the gymnast whose single mum drove him on a 52-mile round trip to the gym each day; Jessica Ennis, of mixed-race, working class stock from Sheffield, is a gold medal winner alongside Anna Watkins and Katherine Grainger, top-class scullers and studying for doctorates. All human life is here, whether it has subsisted on a diet of potatoes and pasta without funding, like Adams, or been fast-tracked to success.

In this context, the memories of the Games have to encompass those who have been excluded from the stadium as well as those lucky enough to get a ticket. Talent exists everywhere, in the estates of Hackney, Haringey and Salford, in suburban homes as well as on the lawns of public schools. If these Olympics are to be more than the bread and circuses claimed by the naysayers, then those gifts must be recognised and encouraged just as fiercely wherever they are found.

If children languishing in difficult circumstances can suddenly feel that they can change their lives, they can dream and have the means to fulfil those dreams, then the legacy of this Games will be immense.

But to do that they don't just need politicians to stop point-scoring and start trying to make a practical difference on the ground in every impoverished and undernourished community. They also need the great silent majority who have revelled in the atmosphere of this Games to assert their sense of what living in a good community means. You nurture ability on the one hand, but on the other you must respect your fellow citizens.

In this sense, the abiding image of London 2012 has not been the triumphant smiles and tears of Bradley Wiggins, Sir Chris Hoy and the victorious cyclists, or the joy of the other medal winners; it has been the great, anonymous mass of volunteers, dressed in unflattering (but strangely welcoming) purple, pink and red, directing visitors around London. Some of the 70,000 have glimpsed the action inside the Olympic venues; others have done nothing more glamorous than direct human traffic at the transport hubs.

But they have done so with resolute cheerfulness and good will, bringing virtues of humour and irony to a task that has made their instructions a million miles from the meaningless "Have a good day". At St Pancras, as the crowds waited for the super-fast Javelin train emblazoned with Rebecca Adlington's name to take them to the Park, a young rail worker shouted through a megaphone: "you will not be allowed on the train without…"

Everyone bristled, waiting for some petty instruction. "…smile on your face". The entire platform broke out laughing.

…

It is a simple enough thing, but it has worked. For the duration of the Olympics, London has put a smile on its face. Britain has begun to remember the country it can be. In the hard times of recession ahead, when we are still trying to build for the future, the real legacy of the Games must be that determination to be generous to each other. Nurture talent, show respect and smile. Not a bad manifesto of memories.

Britain has begun to remember the country it can be

Sarah Crompton, The *Daily Telegraph*, 10 August 2012

Source 2 | Give a life-changing gift this Christmas

As part of its Christmas campaign, the charity Centrepoint asks the reader to think about others and to do something positive to make Christmas better for homeless young people.

http://www.guardian.co.uk/centrepoint

Give a life-changing gift this Christmas

Centrepoint helps homeless and vulnerable young people turn their lives around, not only with the offer of a room at Christmas – but also with practical help, advice and emotional support. Find out how you can support its work during the festive season and beyond.

Share 22
Shout 15
Search 1
Share 0
Email

guardian.co.uk

Print this article

Christmas means different things to different people. For many of us it is a chance to get together with friends and family to enjoy a party, exchange presents, and eat and drink more than we should. For others it is a religious festival of great significance. And for some it is a time away from work, hunkering down in the warmth, and being pleased to stay inside and be cosy. For most of us, fortunately, it is not about being on the streets or alone. It is not about feeling rejected, or scared, or aware that you don't have the love that others do. It is not about facing a family life full of abuse or neglect.

Vulnerable young people, sadly, will be feeling frightened and desperate at Christmas. While most of us will be enjoying a Christmas dinner with loved ones, homeless young people will be cold, hungry and lonely. They also risk being targeted by unscrupulous people who know only too well that homeless young people can be manipulated and exploited. But Centrepoint can help them. This Christmas, as every year, it will provided homeless and vulnerable young people with a warm room for the night. It will also give these young people a Christmas dinner in the company of people who really care about them.

Year-long, Centrepoint helps homeless and vulnerable young people successfully turn their lives around by offering wide-ranging support, including advice on healthcare, education and benefits. Centrepoint also works with other organisations, and lobbies on behalf of young people. It helps vulnerable young people realise that life isn't hopeless and that they have things to look forward to.

In order to help these young people, Centrepoint urgently needs to raise funds this festive season. While you are looking forward to a happy, secure and loving Christmas, why not give something back to those who need it most? What you give will provide a home for Christmas as well as support and practical help for vulnerable young people and make a real difference to their lives.

More on this site

'Now I feel my life is worth something'
Jodie, 20, left her family home to escape the endless arguments, but would have been on the streets without the support of Centrepoint. Here she tells us how the charity has given her the confidence to progress

'A door in a dark period'
Tom, 21, left his home in Glasgow to escape his abusive stepfather, but ended up alone on the streets of London. Here, he tells how Centrepoint is helping him to start afresh

'My life is back on track'
Omar, 24, was forced to leave his home and had nowhere to turn. Here, he tells us how Centrepoint gave him the help and support he needed to become independent and ready for a brighter future

Three ways you can give to Centrepoint this Christmas

One of the best year-round ways of helping young people is through its Sponsor a Room scheme. For a minimum of £12 a month – just 40p a day – paid by direct debit, you could pay for accommodation for a vulnerable young person. Your commitment means that a young person will not only receive somewhere safe to live but also counselling, advice, support, training and essential life skills.

Then there's Centrepoint's Home for Christmas campaign. The organisation seeks one-off cash donations to help get as many young homeless people off the streets and into safe accommodation by Christmas Eve. To do this, Centrepoint needs to raise £306,543 by Christmas Eve to provide 513 homeless young people with a safe place to stay and vital emotional support.

Another way to give is by purchasing one of Centrepoint's virtual gifts as an alternative Christmas present for friends and families. For just £5 you could buy a hot meal for a young person. For £75 you could give an emergency kit, comprising a warm bed for the night, a wash kit and towel, a hot meal, and advice and support. It's the first step towards a new life. You could even give a life-changing £1,600, which would allow a young person to pay for a deposit and first month's rent on a place of their own.

There's much more information about young people, who need your help, Centrepoint's work with them, and ways you can help at centrepoint.org.uk

Source 3 | A letter to… my 14-year-old daughter

Sometimes it is easier to write the words we want to say than actually speak them. In this letter to her daughter, a mother reveals for the first time things about her own past and the choices she had to make.

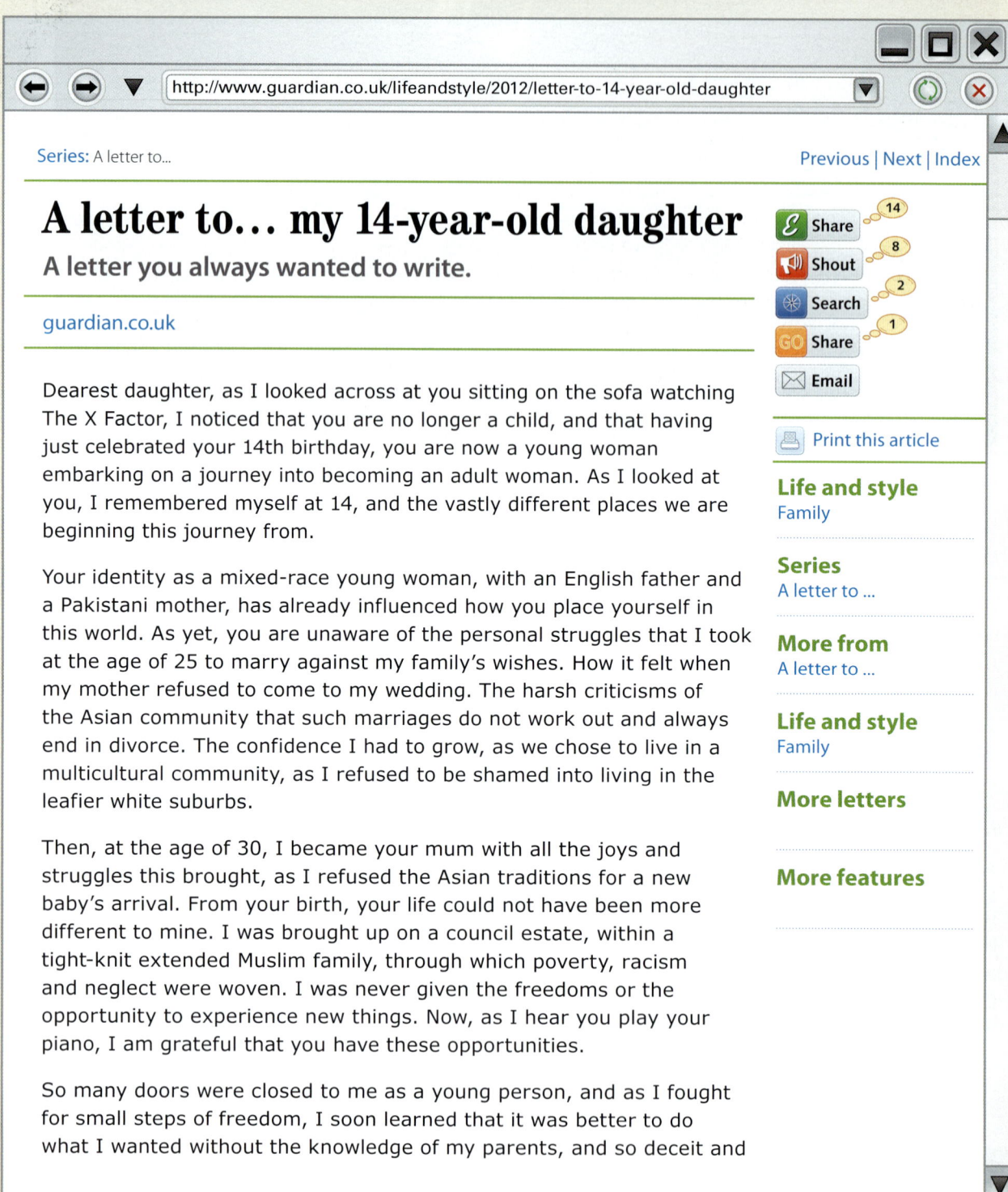

http://www.guardian.co.uk/lifeandstyle/2012/letter-to-14-year-old-daughter

Series: A letter to…   Previous | Next | Index

A letter to… my 14-year-old daughter
A letter you always wanted to write.

guardian.co.uk

Dearest daughter, as I looked across at you sitting on the sofa watching The X Factor, I noticed that you are no longer a child, and that having just celebrated your 14th birthday, you are now a young woman embarking on a journey into becoming an adult woman. As I looked at you, I remembered myself at 14, and the vastly different places we are beginning this journey from.

Your identity as a mixed-race young woman, with an English father and a Pakistani mother, has already influenced how you place yourself in this world. As yet, you are unaware of the personal struggles that I took at the age of 25 to marry against my family's wishes. How it felt when my mother refused to come to my wedding. The harsh criticisms of the Asian community that such marriages do not work out and always end in divorce. The confidence I had to grow, as we chose to live in a multicultural community, as I refused to be shamed into living in the leafier white suburbs.

Then, at the age of 30, I became your mum with all the joys and struggles this brought, as I refused the Asian traditions for a new baby's arrival. From your birth, your life could not have been more different to mine. I was brought up on a council estate, within a tight-knit extended Muslim family, through which poverty, racism and neglect were woven. I was never given the freedoms or the opportunity to experience new things. Now, as I hear you play your piano, I am grateful that you have these opportunities.

So many doors were closed to me as a young person, and as I fought for small steps of freedom, I soon learned that it was better to do what I wanted without the knowledge of my parents, and so deceit and

Share 14
Shout 8
Search 2
Share 1
Email

Print this article

Life and style
Family

Series
A letter to …

More from
A letter to …

Life and style
Family

More letters

More features

deception became woven into my life too. The pressures to conform, to be a "good Muslim" girl and keep the family honour, were suffocating. Behind closed doors at home, the neglect and abuse took place. It was hidden, I felt the shame, lived with the fear and suffered alongside my sister and two younger brothers. Oh, the power we thought our parents had over us! I was convinced that one day my father would indeed beat us so hard that leaving us for dead, he would, as his threats said he would, bury us in the large back garden, and tell the school he had taken us back to Pakistan for good. My sister and I longed for a different blue sky to live under.

As a daughter of immigrant parents, I carried their hopes of a better education for their children – my own veins pulsing with the hard-work ethic and need to be grateful for the opportunity of a free education. And it was education that provided me with the strength to find my own blue sky. I fought to leave home to go to university at the age of 18, and never returned to live with my parents again.

Now as you explore your mixed-race heritage, which I hope we have supported you to do with visits to Pakistan and ensuring you go to multi-cultural schools, I want you to take the very best of all that is Asian with you as you become a woman.

The struggles of identity and belonging will come but I hope that we have given you a strong foundation from which to explore these struggles. All the opportunities and freedoms that I only dreamed of as a young woman, I have offered you. I have chosen a different path of loving you as my daughter, with an unconditional love that many consider "western".

I want you to know that although your journey has been vastly different, I am excited as I watch you standing on the threshold of becoming a woman for all the adventures and possibilities the future holds for you.

May you fly your blue sky with grace, confidence and hope as you find your place in this beautiful and crazy world.

Loving you now and always. *Mum x*

Related

29 Dec 2012
A letter to... my diamond mum and dad

22 Dec 2012
A letter to... my husband's physiotherapist

15 Dec 2012
A letter to... the lady in the next bed

8 Dec 2012
A letter to... my dad, who was the greatest

www.guardian.co.uk, Saturday 3rd November 2012

Source 4 | Disaster

On the 21 October 1966 there was a catastrophic collapse of a colliery slagheap in the Welsh Village of Aberfan, killing 116 children and 28 adults. The following day the Daily Mirror needed only one word to sum up the horror of this event.

Daily Mirror DISASTER

Saturday October 22, 1966   No 19,543

The slag heap swept mercilessly down on the village
Picture by Mirror Cameraman FREDDIE REED

In the words of a little girl of ten

'We heard a noise and we saw all stuff flying about. The room seemed to be flying around. The desks were falling over and the children were shouting and screaming. We couldn't see anything.

But then the dust began to go away. My leg was caught in a desk and could not move, and my arm was hurting. The children were lying all over the place...'

In these words little Dilys Pope last night told the story of the disaster that stunned the nation.

Scores of people died when the gigantic slag heap that brooded over Aberfan, Glamorganshire, swept down into the village to flatten a school and fourteen houses.

Lucky

Dilys lived to tell the tragic story. But she was one of the lucky ones.

Late last night fifty-six bodies had been taken out of the wrecked school. Thirty-six people, mostly children, had been rescued alive. And at least eighty were still buried under the creeping wall of death.

But since no one knows exactly how many people were in the school and the shattered homes, police fear the final death toll may reach 200.

Moving

Hours after the disaster, as more than 2,000 rescuers toiled, and clergymen toured the homes of the stricken relatives, the wall of death was still moving forward, inch by inch.

And South Wales miners' president Glyn Williams said: "The valleys of Wales have seen their tragedies, but never one like this..."

Full Story of the Horror – See Pages 2 and 3
More Pictures – See Pages 9 and 11

Source 5 | A tragedy remembered

Forty years after the Aberfan disaster, survivors recounted their memories of the day and their struggles to come to terms with what happened.

A tragedy remembered: Aberfan, the village that lives in the shadow of the past

Forty years after the landslide in Aberfan that killed 144 people, Barrie Clement finds a community whose grief is still unspoken

Many of the people of Aberfan still cannot bring themselves to speak of it. Forty years on from the disaster some parents, now in their seventies, still secretly hope their children will come home from school. Others tell of the grief and trauma visited on their tiny community by the huge slag heap which slid from a hill above Pantglas junior school, killing 116 children and 28 adults.

Only 25 children survived the catastrophe. Now in their forties and fifties, many still speak of the nightmares and the psychological scarring that afflicts them. The name Aberfan remains synonymous with unspeakable grief about the death of children.

The morning of 21 October 1966 was a typically moist and misty day in the valley near Merthyr Tydfil in south Wales – although the sun shone further up the mountain. The children were in buoyant mood because it was the last day of school before the half-term holiday.

The assembly was shorter than usual. The children sang "All Creatures Great and Small" and then were off to class.

Just before 9.15am they heard a strange rumbling noise. The lights in their classes which hung on long wires from the ceiling began to sway. One teacher said it was probably thunder. In fact a 30ft wave of coal, mud and water was heading for the school. Already it had engulfed a farm cottage in its path, killing all the occupants.

Gaynor Madgwick, then eight years old, remembers that morning vividly. Her mother had to persuade her seven-year-old brother Carl to go to school. He had protested, saying it was not worth it because it was the

last day before the break. Carl and Gaynor's sister Marilyn were killed.

"The first I knew there was something wrong was when I heard a horrific, terrifying rumbling noise getting louder and louder," says Gaynor. "People were frozen to their seats with fright. I tried to run to the door, but then I saw the black coming through the windows. I don't remember anything else until I woke up. I had been impaled at the back of the classroom. Underneath me were two boys who were dead; one was foaming at the mouth, the other's head was cut open."

She found a severed arm on her shoulder. "It was strange. I was convinced it was my brother's arm. He had been in the next classroom, and it gave me a feeling of peace to think it was him. I couldn't see or feel my legs. I think a radiator must have fallen on them.

"I sat there looking at everyone. We'd been engulfed in stuff that had the consistency of cement. It had steam coming off it. I picked up a book called Through the Garden Gate. It was full of blood, but I started to read it."

Eventually rescuers began to appear. "The first person I saw was my granddad. Then I started to cry. I never forgot the look on his face."

Later in hospital, she asked about her brother and sister. "My Dad said they had gone to heaven and my Mum started sobbing."

Aberfan memorial for the 116 children and 28 adults who died in the 1966 disaster.

In common with many other survivors she did not talk about that day for years. "There was no counselling in those days and people assumed because we were children we were resilient, but we were suffering." When she was a teenager, however, Gaynor underwent psychiatric treatment – even then, neither she nor the town were ready. "That was humiliating. It was a stigma back then."

The tragedy continues to have a devastating effect on those involved. "Some have died young, some have been constantly depressed. Some have been in and out of psychiatric hospital. One person has become a recluse. Most people have handled it by not talking about it, but I don't think that's the right approach," she says.

The winter Laurie Lee, who visited Aberfan a year after the disaster, later remarked that the surviving children were part of the "unhealed scar tissue of Aberfan". That is still true.

In Jeff Edwards' class, only four of the 34 children survived. Jeff, then eight, was saved because he was trapped in a pocket of air. "I remember waking up and there was a dead girl across my shoulder. Her face started to puff out, but one eye seemed to be sinking into her head. There were screams and shouts to begin with, but the sounds got less and less.

"When I was being rescued I remember saying that I wanted to take my felt-tip pens with me, but they said 'Bugger your felt tip pens', and I was thrown from one rescuer to another. I was finally taken out of the building at about 11 o'clock.

I was the last one to come out alive.

"I was examined by doctors and wrapped in a red blanket. Even now in hospitals I shudder when I see them."

Jeff was treated for head and stomach injuries, but the real injury was the long-term psychological impact. "It can be very burdensome. It can close you down for a couple of days. I have to go to bed until it's over. I get irritable and depressed. You can get bouts of guilt for surviving while others were killed. But those seem to be the classic symptoms of anybody who has been involved in disasters."

Clearly Jeff still needs someone to explain to him why he survived and others died: "Many people can't talk about it. It upsets them too much. The huge emotional waves can be uncontrollable. Even after 40 years some people are still waiting for their children to come home."

Despite the emotional burden, Jeff went on from Pantglas to the London School of Economics and a City accountancy firm. He returned to the area to become an independent councillor, and eventually mayor of Merthyr.

At the time of the disaster, there were some 100,000 miners in south Wales, an area which relied heavily on the coal and steel industries. Today there are a few hundred miners left. Most of the pits – like Merthyr Vale colliery, which produced the Aberfan slag heap – have been "landscaped". One has been turned into a museum.

Pit closures under the Thatcher government ripped the heart out of the Merthyr area. At one stage nearly 30 per cent of the able-bodied were out of work, while the other adults were registered disabled largely through industrial diseases.

Aberfan was once the archetypal monochrome industrial village, with mountains stripped bare of deciduous trees to feed the furnaces of nearby ironworks and black patches of coal visible where grass struggled to grow. Now the hills are carpeted in Forestry Commission conifers, the village is brightly painted and cars are parked outside most homes.

And yet the Aberfan disaster still haunts this part of Wales. Apart from the deep emotional scars, there is a legacy which is causing considerable bitterness – although it is a word that local people prefer to avoid.

There is an unresolved conflict over reparation. A reluctant National Coal Board, which denied responsibility for the catastrophically unstable slag heap, was forced to pay compensation. Lord Robens, the board's chairman, claimed that his officials were unaware of the stream that ran through the tip and liquefied its contents so disastrously. The stream appeared on the Ordnance Survey map of the locality.

After much wrangling the sum of £500 was paid to those involved, and £1,000 to those who had lost one or more children [...].

Some, including Gaynor, believe that additional compensation is due to those whose lives were irreversibly affected [...].

Barrie Clement, *The Independent*, Saturday 21 October 2006

Source 6 | Hurray for teenagers

Teenagers often get a bad press but, in this feature article, Louisa Young questions whether such negative views of young people are deserved.

Hurray for teenagers

Why are people so negative about teenagers, asks Louisa Young, when most of them are adorable, funny, interesting, imaginative, brave, generous, loyal, hard-working and helpful?

Why are so many people so negative about teenagers and so rude to them? I'm not talking about the ones who knife each other at bus stops and torment each other to suicide on social networking websites, about whom we read so much in the scared and scaremongering newspapers. I'm talking about everyday, normal teenagers. There is scarcely another group in the country so stereotyped and maligned.

What is worse, most adults think that teenagers deserve the bad press they get. I don't, so I am going to upend the negative generalisations and announce my own: that teenagers are, in general, adorable, funny, energetic, very hard-working, beautiful, interesting, imaginative, generous, loyal, vulnerable, brave, charming, helpful, clever, well-dressed and very good cooks. (And I'm just talking about my own. I'm writer in residence at two inner London secondary schools.)

Consider these teenagers. Eighteen-year-old soldiers William Aldridge, Joseph Murphy and James Backhouse, died in July in Afghanistan trying to save the lives of their brother in arms. Andrew Dalton, 17, from Wirral, saved two small children from a fire. Mike Perham, 17, sailed round the world alone. Fifteen-year-old Tom Daley is a world champion diver. Milan Karki, 18, in Nepal has invented a new kind of solar panel using human hair. Welsh 15-year-olds Leighton Griffiths and Tyler Hulpin saved six children from the burning house next door in May. Leighton went back in three times and ended up in hospital himself.

★ ★ ★

Of course, not every teenager gets the opportunity to be that kind of hero. But in my experience they are not lazy sods who never get out of bed.

Milan Karki

Isabel, a 16-year-old London A-Level student about whom I can say nothing because she is my own daughter, worked out an average teenage schoolday for me: "Up at 6.30am, leave at 7.45am for school at 8.30am; out again at 4pm, extra curricular stuff til 5pm, home 5.45pm, three hours of homework, say, takes you to 8.45pm, by which time, if you're to get the recommended nine and a half hours' sleep, you should go to bed."

But they also need to eat (family meals round the table, five vegetables a day!); to exercise (obesity!); to wash (dirty!); to maintain their beauty (munter!). They must do chores (spoilt!); get out of the house (couch potato!) but not hang out in public places (threatening! antisocial! Or, er, dangerous!) And perhaps they might also be allowed a bit of social life…

How on earth can they fit it all in? Teenagers do, physically, need around nine and a half hours sleep a night, during which new brain cells are wired, thus increasing intelligence, self-awareness and performance. They get on average about seven hours, whereupon they often become cranky, slower-witted and resentful.

Russell Foster, chair of circadian neuroscience at Brasenose College, Oxford, has shown that teenagers' brains work better during the afternoon. They're not lazy; they're biologically programmed. There are simple reasons why they never clean up. First they haven't the time. Second, nobody clears up as much as someone else might want them to. Third, they aren't usually as good at it as adults. They haven't had the practice.

★ ★ ★

But these are petty annoyances, compared with the big moans. And these are the ones where we really do them injustice. For example, drinking. If they do drink like fish, where do they get the idea? Who makes the booze? And who makes the money out of it? Not teenagers. A society that drinks as much as we do and still advertises alcohol, even after the British Medical Association has told us not to, is a society that might benefit from doing one of those alcohol-awareness questionnaires. Shouting at teenagers for getting drunk is a simple projection of our own faults on to people we feel we can boss around.

Alongside this are the parents who think they are "best friends" with their teenagers. No, you're not. They've got loads

of friends and only one or two parents. This is, of course, no reason not to be friendly[...].

Because we have created a terrifying world, and we feel guilty, we keep them home and let them watch TV all day, whereupon they get fat from lack of movement, and succumb to the horrible fantasy world of advertising, where clever people make fortunes deluding us into spending money we don't have on things we don't need. Which is much more dangerous.

And then we start castigating them for being greedy little label-made consumerists.

Not knowing your own worth, particularly among girls (at whom most of these ads are aimed) is a fundamental contributor to promiscuity. The image of promiscuous teenagers is another at which too many adults gawp in combined envy and horror. But they grow, as Rumi, the 13th-century Sufi poet said, in the garden in which they are planted. They imitate adults, and look to what they see glorified and lo, they think nothing is more glamorous than falling in and out of cabs with their knickers showing, though this goes against the inner natural reserve of many, which is honoured in anything they see around them. Instead, they see quasi-pornography in adverts and real pornography on the internet,[...] and they become confused as to what is required of them.

★ ★ ★

No wonder, perhaps that adults are scared of them. But, as organisations such as Kids Company know, the really scary ones are the really scared ones. The best thing an adult can do is find a way past the scary behaviour of the scared kid. You don't have to hug the hoodies lurking in your street, but you could try saying "Evening, lads." I asked some teenagers if they are badly behaved. "Everyone expects you to rebel," says Kehinde, a 6ft, 16-year-old karate black belt with the voice of an angel and a cute afro, "so people go along with it because it you don't, other teenagers reject you, because they are scared of being rejected."

Everybody wants to fit in; everybody wants to stand out. "The worst thing," says Ruby, 17, an art scholar, is that "some of us act exactly how we want because we are teenagers, but others feel as if they should act a certain way to be a teenager."

"It's a vicious circle," agrees Sindri, 16. "People say, 'Oh, she's weird', to make themselves look not weird. To look bigger by putting someone else down. I hate it."

If they do want to be good, they get rounded on again. My nephew Remel, 13 says: "Once a year you see all these late-teens achieving amazing GCSE results, but for most of the time teenagers are portrayed in a bad light by the media. Stabbings, shootings. They seem to miss out that not all teenagers are carrying around knives and thinking they own the place. Yet when there is a chance for the good majority of the teenage population to be shown, we are portrayed as generally terrible."

When teenagers do get good results – well, the standards have fallen, haven't they?

Possibly the rudest thing adults do to teenagers is to assume they are always trying to steal from shops. Some are and, of course, they shouldn't. But can we bear in mind that they are constantly being told that particular items are 'must haves' and led to believe that possession is the source of all joy? Everyone I've spoken to for this article has been followed round a shop by the store detective at least once.

I think there is an insidious tendency to moan about our own children in order not to appear smug. [...] If this is the case, we are making a big error.[...] Would we belittle our friends? I think not. [...] Our teenagers still, more than ever, on that long journey from childhood to adulthood, want, need and deserve our encouragement and admiration.

Louisa Young, www.guardian.co.uk, Saturday 5 December 2009

Source 7 | One perfect hour with Uganda's mountain gorillas

Extracts from books are sometimes printed in magazines and newspapers. They cross the boundary of non-fiction and journalism. In the following such extract, a zoologist comes face to face with a mountain gorilla.

One perfect hour with Uganda's mountain gorillas

In an extract from his latest book, zoologist and TV presenter Mark Carwardine describes the unique frisson of meeting mountain gorillas.

You only get an hour. And there's an awful lot of travelling and trekking to be done beforehand. But that hour is likely to be one of the most emotional, humbling and exhilarating of your life. Rubbing shoulders with wild mountain gorillas is a true privilege and, if everyone could do it just once, the world would be a better place.

The business of gorilla tourism is a vexed one. I know people who have always wanted to see gorillas, but have worried that tourism might be causing disturbance or exposing the animals to human disease. But in truth the gorillas probably wouldn't be here at all without tourism. It is the one thing that can guarantee their survival, by making them worth more alive than dead – to governments and local people alike.

There are currently about 800 mountain gorillas left in Africa: 480 in the Virunga Volcanoes, which straddle Uganda, Rwanda and the Democratic Republic of Congo (DRC), and some 310–340 in Bwindi Impenetrable Forest, Uganda.

The Virunga Volcanoes is the place most people imagine when they think of mountain gorillas. Thirty-six family groups (and 14 solitary silverbacks) are distributed across three different protected areas: Volcanoes National Park in Rwanda; Mgahinga Gorilla National Park in Uganda; and Virunga National Park in the DRC. But the gorilla-watching opportunities are actually quite limited. It's a little hit-and-miss in the DRC because, unhappily, the animals have been caught in a vortex of human conflict and misery and are forced to share their home with a motley collection of rebels and heavily armed soldiers.

Meanwhile, the only habituated group in Uganda's Mgahinga has a reputation for

mature male or 'silverback' along with his harem of several females, various immature 'blackback' males and youngsters.

Every morning, the latest influx of tourists gathers on the lawns near the forest entrance for a detailed briefing, before setting off chaperoned by trackers, guides, armed guards and porters.

The super-human porters will carry anything – no amount of camera equipment is too much. The trek can take anything from less than an hour (if you're lucky) to as long as 11 hours (if you're not). It all depends on where your allotted gorilla family happens to be at the time.

Within minutes of entering the forest you are sweating and panting, crawling and clambering your way along slippery paths and precipitous mountain tracks. The dark, wet Impenetrable Forest is aptly named – it's a riot of green where things grow on top of other things that grow on top of more things in layers of ferns, mosses, creepers and lichens. In places, the forest is so thick you have to hike on solid mats of vegetation that tremble and flex with every step, threatening to break through and dump you into the unseen depths below.

It's all very exciting. And the moment you come face-to-face with your first gorilla, the mud and sweat become distant memories. Standing in the heart of a seemingly limitless jungle, with a family of the largest primates in the world, is one of life's greatest pleasures. Your allotted hour – the maximum time allowed – goes so quickly. But life will never be quite the same again.

Mark Carwardine, *Wanderlust*: Issue 128, April 2012

crossing the border into Rwanda and the DRC, so it is not a reliable spot for viewing either. That leaves Volcanoes National Park in Rwanda, which has eight habituated gorilla groups and is generally considered to be the hotspot for gorilla-watching.

But I really like lesser-known Bwindi Impenetrable Forest, a discrete area some 30km to the north. Bwindi is a tiny island of 330 sq km of equatorial primeval rainforest, surrounded by a sea of banana and tea plantations. A vast, misty, mountainous jungle, it is one of the most biologically diverse places in the world.

Although it can be difficult to spot much wildlife through the mass of huge trees festooned with vines and creepers, this forest is home to no fewer than 120 species of mammal, 360 species of birds, 310 types of butterflies and 1,000 different flowering plants. As you walk the trails, you are greeted by a cacophony of animal sounds at every turn.

But mountain gorillas are obviously the star attraction. The Uganda Wildlife Authority has habituated seven gorilla families to receive human visitors. These consist of as few as seven animals to as many as 36, led by a

Source 8 | 3.56 am: man steps on to the moon

History was made on 20 July 1969 when Neil Armstrong became the first man to step onto the surface of the moon. Extraordinary photographs and detailed reports filled the front pages of all the newspapers.

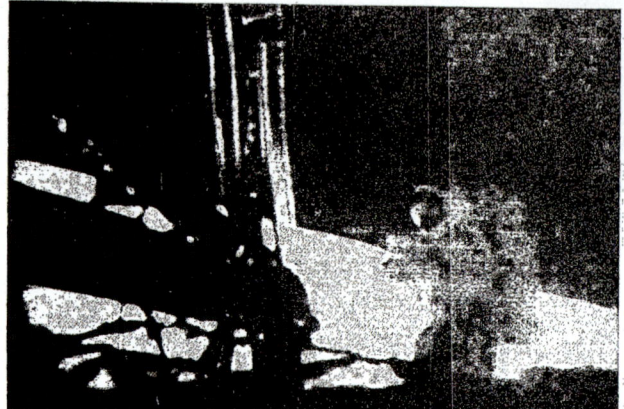

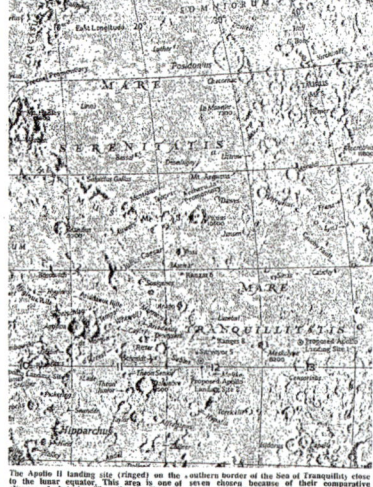

See page 85 for full text.

Men are on the moon.

At 3.56 this morning Armstrong stepped from the lunar module and set foot on lunar ground. It was the fulfilment of a dream which men have shared since the beginning of recorded history. Aldrin followed his commander down the steps of the lander – already named Tranquillity Base – 19 minutes later.

3.56 am: man steps on to the moon

Armstrong reported that the surface seemed to be a very fine powder into which his feet sank about one-eighth of an inch. He could see his footprints clearly.

Armstrong's first words on the moon were: "That's one small step for man. One giant leap for mankind." The first television view millions on earth saw was Armstrong's foot descending slowly. Then there was his full figure.

"It's a very soft surface, but here and there where I poke with the sample collector I run into a very hard surface," he said. "It appears to be the same material." The moon "has a harsh beauty all its own," Aldrin reported. "It looks like a desert of the United States, but it is very beautiful."

Aldrin experimented with movement in the low gravity, and remarked that a moonwalker had to be careful to lean in the direction he wanted to go or he would lurch around "like someone slightly inebriated." When they started to examine their surroundings Aldrin reported finding a purple rock.

"That's one small step for man. One giant leap for mankind."

The decision to walk early was made three hours after the lunar module Eagle had made a perfect landing at 9 17 p.m. four miles downrange from the chosen site. The spacecraft was steered manually to clear a boulder-strewn crater "the size of a football field." It was a moment of extraordinary tension and silence. The lunar module curved gently down over the Sea of Tranquillity, its drama heightened by the calm, almost casual voices of the astronauts and the mission controller at Houston.

The landing was perfect. Spaceflight Centre and the world seemed momentarily stunned by emotion: only Armstrong, Aldrin and – above them – Collins seemed unmoved. "You got a bunch of guys who are turning blue who can start breathing again," said the Houston space controller.

…

Every step of the preparation for landing yesterday went smoothly. Armstrong and Aldrin transferred from the command module code-named Columbia – to the lunar module Eagle during the tenth orbit and on the eleventh orbit Glynn Lunney, the flight controller at Houston, told the world that all spacecraft systems were "operating just fine."

Anthony Tucker, *The Guardian*,
Monday 21 July 1969

Source 9 | How technology is taking over our children's lives

Is it the children or their parents who are addicted to technology. Here, Rowan Pelling investigates where the blames lies.

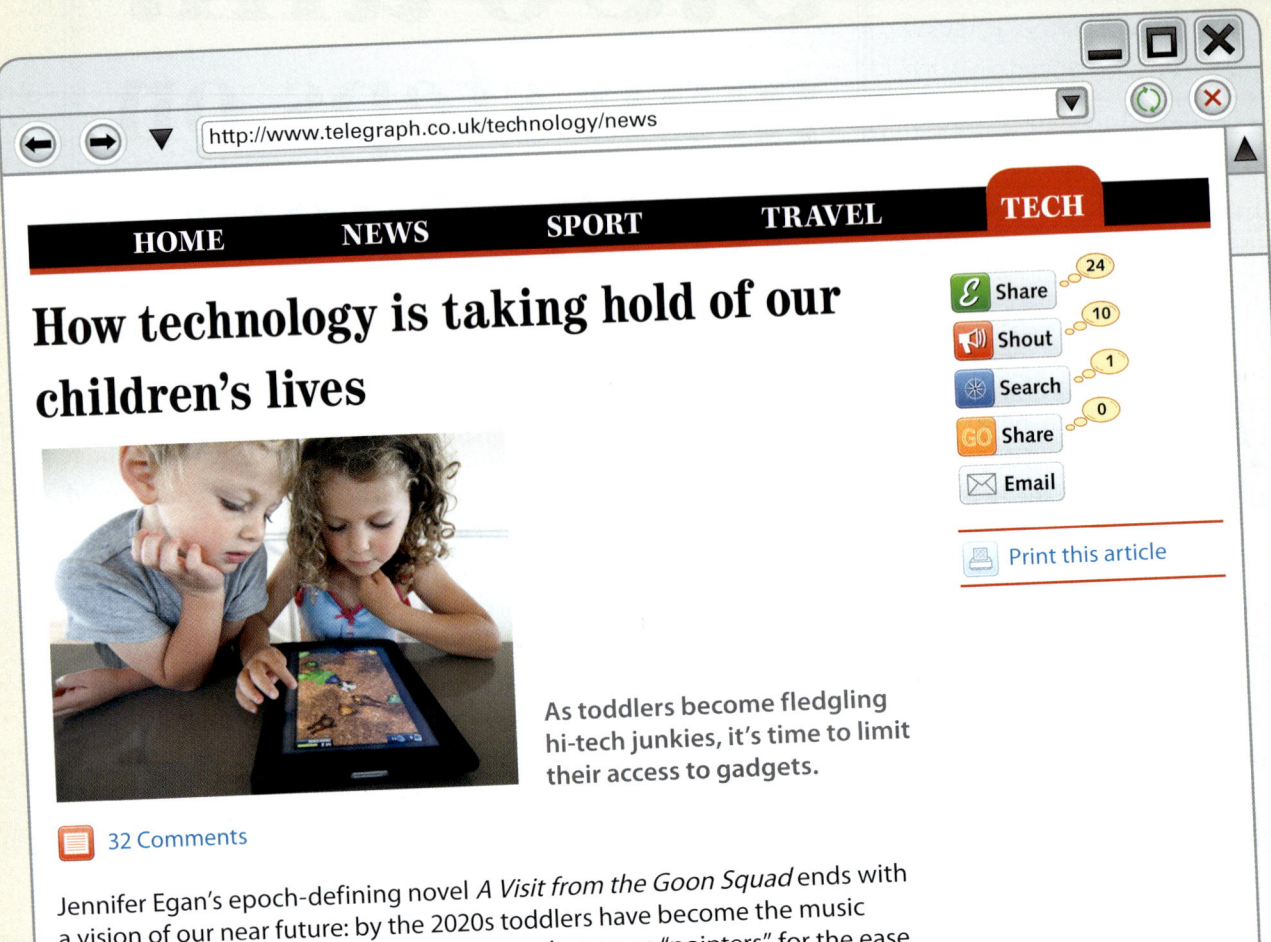

http://www.telegraph.co.uk/technology/news

HOME   NEWS   SPORT   TRAVEL   **TECH**

How technology is taking hold of our children's lives

As toddlers become fledgling hi-tech junkies, it's time to limit their access to gadgets.

Share 24
Shout 10
Search 1
Share 0
Email

Print this article

32 Comments

Jennifer Egan's epoch-defining novel *A Visit from the Goon Squad* ends with a vision of our near future: by the 2020s toddlers have become the music industry's most influential consumer group, known as "pointers" for the ease with which they download tracks via touch screens. One critic told me she found this final chapter "implausible". She wouldn't have said that, I replied, had she had a toddler in her house.

It's commonplace now to see tots who can't talk, but can navigate an iPhone with ease, or infants who scowl when they touch a computer screen that doesn't respond with the immediate elasticity of an iPad. These fledgling hi-tech junkies are, of course, reflections of their Wi-Fi-zombie mums and dads. I can't be the only parent who has, on occasion, conducted an entire conversation with a child without once tearing my eyes away from a screen – leading my younger son to shout, "You're not looking at me, Mummy!"

Granted, I work from home and my laptop is the tool of my trade, but I can't avoid the guilty realisation that my computer can seem, at times, even more compelling than my offspring – or, at least, less demanding. I am equally aware that the TV sometimes makes a convenient au pair. It's small wonder a psychologist, Aric Sigman, this week warned of the perils of "passive parenting" and "benign neglect" caused by our reliance on gadgets. Indeed, Sigman's presentation to members of the Royal College of Paediatrics and Child Health outlined the parallels between screen dependency and alcohol and drug addiction [...].

Not that you need to be a research scientist to realise how addictive the virtual world can be. When I'm bidding for junk on eBay, all semblance of sanity flies out of the window; my hands sweat, my heartbeat surges and I truly feel like I've "won" that item, even though I've just parted with £200 and I don't need a rocking horse. So I'm with Sigman when he says screen dependency poses high risks to children's mental and physical health and their access to such gadgets should be restricted [...].

All around us we observe the behaviour-altering sway of new technology on adults, so it seems astounding that anyone wouldn't fret about its influence on developing brains. Walk past any bus stop and you will see grown people so disconnected from one another that they might as well be in Perspex boxes, as they angrily jab at tiny keypads or talk to the air. Go to a restaurant and you will see diners so addicted to their "CrackBerries" that every social nicety is ignored in pursuit of staying connected. I was on a plane last week where three people seated near me filmed the landing views on their smart phones, in preference to actually looking at them [...].

It seems to me alcohol's hold on society is as nothing to the manic grip of digital technology, and we're not handing booze out indiscriminately to our young. So aren't we right to fret when we see the hypnotised look that comes over our children's faces when they spend too long on the computer? My eight-year-old's glazed expression when he plays his favourite Bin Weevils (on his father's computer, supervised, twice weekly) is radically different from the lively cognitive whirrings glimpsed when he draws, or writes stories, or builds Lego cities. Only an idiot need be told there's a great difference between hewing out your own imaginative realm or, at the push of a button, entering a virtual world created for you. The latter is seductive in its easy accessibility, and corrupting for the same reason.

I'm not advocating prohibition: like most addictive pursuits, the online world has many upsides, and our children will be part of the digital revolution in a way that we're only just beginning to comprehend. I wouldn't want either of my sons to be isolated from their peers. But I do believe that Sigman is right when he calls for children's viewing time to be heavily restricted. Even adults should exercise restraint. Where's the evidence? Google boss Eric Schmidt told an audience of students at Boston University last Sunday that they should put down their gadgets for at least an hour every day: "Take your eyes off that screen and look into the eyes of the person you love. Have a conversation, a real conversation." And if he doesn't know what he's talking about, no one does.

Related articles

23 May 2012
Graphic: UK children more likely to be 'illiterate' than Australian or Canadian children, despite higher spending

21 May 2012
Facebook denies plans to open up site to under-13s

17 May 2012
Mps call for video game ban

Add a comment   Comment with a Telegraph account

Login | Register with the Telegraph

Rowan Pelling, www.telegraph.co.uk,
Tuesday 22 May 2012

Source 10 | Skyfall Reviews

Whether it's a concert, film, book or game that interests you, one of the best places to check it out is the review section of a paper or magazine. You may not agree with the writer but you cannot claim you have not been warned!

Time Out says:

Were you expecting an exploding pen? We don't really go in for that anymore.' That's Ben Whishaw's Q to Daniel Craig's James Bond in 'Skyfall' – a Bond movie that boldly struts forward while looking back over its shoulder to the past. That's what the 007 films are all about – an evolving mix of tradition and progress – and here we have director Sam Mendes ('American Beauty', 'Revolutionary Road') bringing to the franchise a stately look, sombre mood and ample room to breathe. Saying that, the fiftieth anniversary of the 007 movie project demands the odd knowing wink, to the likes of the classic Aston Martin DB5 from 'Goldfinger' and even the crocodiles that Roger Moore hops across in 'Live and Let Die'.

The Bond films are savvy magpies, smartly pinching the shiniest, newest jewels of moviemaking for themselves [...] 'Skyfall' takes its cues not only from the current, moodier breed of superhero movies, but also from the world around us. There are nods to terrorism, data theft, hacking and even attention-grabbing government inquiries – but nothing is specific or exact enough to mean anything significant. This is a Bond movie: atmosphere is all. The appearance of contemporary relevance is enough.

The story sees Bond in an emotional crisis after a failed mission to Istanbul leaves the names of secret agents in the hands of an unknown villain. Trips to Shanghai and Macau follow as 007 pulls himself together and tries to find the culprit for Judi Dench's M and Ralph Fiennes's Mallory, her Whitehall superior. There's trouble at home, too, as a bomb explodes in the MI6 building in London and it becomes clear that M is under threat.

Meanwhile, a delicious foe emerges in Silva (Javier Bardem), a camp, creepy and smooth character who dares to challenge Bond's masculinity in an arresting scene in which his hands run up 007's legs. But the film's many commercial sponsors can rest easy: Craig's harried, stern Bond is as inscrutable and wordless as ever. He has plenty of welcome one-liners ('I'm just changing carriages,' he quips, leaping from the roof of one train car to the next), but delivers them like someone cracking gags at a funeral.

'Skyfall' is a highly distinctive Bond movie. It has some stunning visual touches: motorbikes racing along the roof of Istanbul's Grand Bazaar; the neon playing off the precipitous glass of a skyscraper in Shanghai; the Scottish landscapes of its bleak finale. Also, it mostly manages to convince us that there's something at stake by giving a hint of Bond's emotional life beyond this story: rooting his crisis in his relationship (or lack of) with his parents, without coming on too heavy-handed or pleading with the psychology.

Mendes knows there's a risk of coming over po-faced by omitting the traditional pleasures of a Bond movie, and his approach seems calculated to stick to the formula while moving things forward. Still, the role of the Bond girls, played by Naomie Harris as an MI6 colleague and Bérénice Marlohe as a femme fatale, feel token and underwhelming. The tourism element of 'Skyfall' – especially the Macau section – is awkward too.

It's only in the second half of the film, which takes place entirely in the UK, that you get the feeling that Mendes has played the compulsory 007 cards that any Bond director has to. Now he's properly able to get stuck into a more punchy, more unified mix of action, emotion and story that climaxes in a fittingly isolated and lonely final showdown between Bond and his latest nemesis.

Dave Calhoun, *Time Out*, Thursday 21 July 2012

Back with a bang: Skyfall could go down as the best Bond ever

It is full-on exhilaration as it criss-crosses the globe from one stunning action sequence to the next before settling down in the wilds of Scotland for its gripping climax

★★★★★ **Five star rating**

★ THE STARS ★

Daniel Craig, Judi Dench, Javier Bardem, Naomie Harris, Bérénice Marlohe, Ralph Fiennes, Ben Whishaw.

★ THE STORY ★

When Bond's assignment goes badly wrong, MI6 is attacked and M (Dench) has to relocate the agency. Bond (Craig) heads to Shanghai and then Macau on the trail of Silva (Bardem), who plans to come after M to avenge a wrong done during the Hong Kong handover.

★ THE VERDICT ★

Skyfall could go down as the best Bond ever. It is full-on exhilaration as it criss-crosses the globe from one stunning action sequence to the next before settling down in the wilds of Scotland for its gripping climax.

He may be 50 in Bond years, but there is no denying that the world's greatest agent is still in tip-top form, with Skyfall delivering the right amount of guns, girls and gadgets to keep fans happy.

In 1962, a new hero was unveiled to the film world, and while it has been an up-and-down ride over the years, this 23rd official movie is action-packed, cleverly scripted, beautifully shot and establishes Daniel Craig as a true Bond. The film opens in spectacular form with a chase through Istanbul and on the roof of a speeding train, before heading to a Shanghai dripping in neon for a brilliantly brutal fight scene.

But, unusually for a Bond film, perhaps the majority of the action takes place in the UK, with Bond pounding the London streets in pursuit of killers who have M in their sights.

Some new characters – Ben Whishaw as a nerdy Q, Naomie Harris as field agent Eve, and Ralph Fiennes as a politician – join the roster, while Judi Dench has her best outing yet as M. Plus they are all up against a charismatic villain in the form of Silva, with Javier Bardem relishing playing the bad guy.

From gunplay and giant reptiles through to Bond girls battling it out for the best evening dress award, Skyfall has it all.

Mark Adams, The *Mirror*, 21 October 2012

Source 11 | Japan earthquake and tsunami

Disasters and their consequences feature strongly in the world of journalism. Here, one man recounts his experiences when a devastating earthquake and tsunami hit the east coast of Japan.

Japan earthquake and tsunami: 'we had no idea how much worse it would get

Henry Green *talks to Carin Nakanishi, an intern at a Tokyo architect firm when Japan was hit by March's devastating earthquake.*

On 11 March this year, the eastern coast of Japan was hit by the most powerful earthquake in its history. The subsequent tsunami caused a series of nuclear meltdowns which have poisoned food and water supplies and left countless people with radiation sickness. Almost 16,000 people died in the disaster, although many remain unaccounted for. Henry Green interviewed Carin Nakanishi, a Japanese student who was in Tokyo during the disaster.

Thirty hours later I would be standing in a supermarket wearing a mask and sunglasses, hoarding supplies for a nuclear meltdown. But at one o'clock I was on my lunch break. I was interning with a team of Tokyo architects and, with two Swiss and Canadian friends, was sampling a new cafe. We spent an hour tasting each other's pasta and discussing plans for our night out.

The biggest earthquake in Japan's history.

Back in the office, I was making models when the first tremors started. I put my craft knife down as the whole room felt the smallest of shakes, and people started murmuring about an earthquake. The tremors grew stronger but there was no screaming and nobody really seemed to panic. Looking around me, I saw three walls stacked to the ceiling with objects that could potentially fall on me so I moved to the nearest table. I wanted to take cover underneath it, but felt too stupid to cower under there while everybody else stood calmly by their desks. [...] My survival instinct, screaming at me to run and hide, felt ridiculous compared to the calmness of the other people in the office. It was even more terrifying glancing out the window and seeing the adjacent building move in the opposite direction, while the electric wires swayed like trees in a hurricane. Then, just like it had started, the tremors receded and finally stopped altogether.

★★★

Not knowing what to do, I returned to the office, and to my model.

Then, it started all over again. Having taken up my post by the table, I was told by a colleague to hold up a shelf, as files were falling from it. Again, disregarding my instinct and all logic, I did as the others were doing: holding up inanimate objects that could potentially kill us. The shaking gradually grew more violent, and we had no idea how much worse it would get. The idea that we had somehow sailed out of a storm suddenly seemed ridiculous. There was no storm to sail out of: the Earth was spasming beneath our feet, and we were pretty much vulnerable as long as we were touching it.

★ ★ ★

A tsunami had been mentioned shortly after the first earthquake. I asked if it had come already and if people would be OK. Those in my office laughed and said, "Of course!"

No one could have guessed what was happening a few hundred kilometres further north. The phone lines were down and news was trickling through websites, but we refused to believe the first videos we saw of the wave swallowing a van. But it must have happened because of the earthquake we had all felt. The fact that it was the biggest earthquake in Japan's history reached us. I looked out the window but pedestrians were going about their errands as before. Everyone's main concern seemed to be facing Tokyo's rush hour without any public transport.

Using Facebook, I'd managed to contact a family friend who agreed to pick me up. Most people, however, were making their four-hour walk home along crowded pavements. I had invited my fellow interns, as they could not understand a single word on the news and were equally shaken. Everyone lightened up as we hurtled through Tokyo in a vintage Ferrari. [...] The novelty of the journey distracted us from what had happened and we went home blissfully unaware of what was really going on.

As soon as I walked into my house, this illusion was broken. Strangely for a Japanese house, everyone was wearing their shoes inside, and had their coats on. Their ashen faces told of the real disaster hitting Japan. Every TV channel was broadcasting the same harrowing footage of about 600 people on the roof of an evacuation building, surrounded by fire and flood water. The authorities were powerless to help, and we watched on as tragedy ensued. It is that image that will stick with me longest. There was an awful realisation that those people burning in an office block had felt the same violent throes as us, the same initial calm, and, but for a few hundred kilometres, their story could have been ours.

★ ★ ★

The next day, I knew turning on the news would only bring worse stories. But the inexplicable explosion at Fukushima could not have been predicted. The news programmes were broadcasting it two hours after it had happened, and we had no idea how quickly the radiation would reach Tokyo. No useful information was being offered by the government or the media, so we prepared ourselves with instructions from the internet. Wearing wet masks, covering every inch of our bodies and wearing non-fibrous clothing that we would discard before re-entering the house, we set off to buy enough supplies in case we couldn't leave the house again.

★ ★ ★

The next morning, the never-ending nightmare seemed to worsen. Rain was predicted on Monday, which would have brought the radiation to Tokyo, so we locked up our house and were on a train to Kyoto in the west within few hours. The sense of relief when arriving in Kyoto is indescribable. The knot in my chest loosened, the shops were fully stocked, and the residents hadn't even felt any tremors. A few days later I flew back to London, where I live, but had nothing to take as I had realised nothing is really necessary in an emergency.

However, I did take the memory of those few days with me. My body would react to the slightest vibration, be it a car driving past my window or a Starbucks fridge. The world's media has moved on from Japan, but this disaster is not over. The psychological scars that millions of others have will hopefully heal. But food supplies are ruined and children have been exposed to radiation.

The Earth was spasming beneath our feet.

In so many ways, this disaster was not mine. So many people died and lost their entire families, that to pretend otherwise would be crude and insensitive, but it is important that these stories continue to be shared. Like the quake itself, the tsunami and subsequent meltdowns have had severe aftershocks, and there's no certainty that Japan will recover from it.

Henry Green, the *Guardian*, Friday 12th August 2011

Source 12 | Photographs of the Japan earthquake and tsunami damage

Sometimes, to see is to believe. Photographs illustrate and enhance an article showing us scenes that words cannot capture.

A

B

Source 13 | Don McCullin: Celebrated War Photographer

Without the journalistic photographer many articles would lack interest and appeal; it is a job that carries responsibilities, anxieties and regrets.

Don McCullin:
celebrated war photographer on the value of his craft

Don McCullin is one of the most celebrated living war photographers having covered conflicts from Iraq to Vietnam, from Bristol to Lebanon. Yet despite spending countless decades covering revolutions, famines, wars and poverty, the 76-year-old is not sure if war photography has achieved that much.

Q How do you judge if you've done a good job?

A I have judged my achievements and the fact is they brought very little. Every year there is another war, as there is this year with the Arab Spring, costing hundreds and hundreds of lives. Look at Syria – only on the weekend President Assad issued a warning that if you meddle with us, there'll be Armageddon. What good are all these war reportings? What have they achieved? Nothing.

Q But it is important to document these things, to bear witness?

A It can be another leaf of history, but they don't change anything. Don't expect change, just because you've recorded it.

Q What about influencing 'hearts and minds'?

A Some people react, but what can they do about it? It's about governments. They have the power to change, not the man in the street. I came to realise this 20 years ago. Each year there are new wars, new famines, new tragedies. You can't blame my pessimism, can you?

Q Do you not see the value of it any more?

A I don't, to be honest. It might seem a rather tragic statement from someone who spent so long doing it. I also take pictures of people living in poverty here [UK], people living in shop doorways. There is value in that. With our society we can change the quality of our existence. We can change poverty here and slum housing, but not getting involved on the other side of the globe in cultures with different beliefs.

Q How has the job changed?

A The eighties was a time of change, with a serious profitability drive. I was at the Sunday Times and I left because they made it plain that the magazine was going to be a money-spinner. I was basically forced out and into the wilderness for a while. The advertising boys didn't want adverts next to dying children and they won.

It's also difficult these days when you're embedded with an army because they try to corral you all the time. It started in Iraq. They don't want you running all over the battlefield, seeing whatever you want to see. They have an agenda; they suffocate your ambitions. They don't want you getting hurt, but they also don't want pictures of dead American soldiers.

Q How does people taking pictures with mobile phones, filming and publishing their own images affect your profession?

A I'd like to know why there was no press around when they captured Gaddafi. I can't figure out why it was only the murderers with the mobile phones there. The press was probably around but being held back. I haven't seen one powerful picture come out of Libya, not one. When you see those pictures, the quality is so bad.

Q Though from a shock perspective, that footage of Gaddafi dying was just as potent, even if it was badly shot?

A It was out of focus, in the heat of the frenzy prior to his death, but yes, it was almost like a Van Gogh. You could see the terror in his face even in that poor reproduction.

Q Does mainstream media have to keep up with graphic pictures, such as Gaddafi's final moments, on the internet?

A Publications aren't that interested in keeping up on that front because the celebrity agenda is where the money is. They are all just happy to run those mobile phone pictures of Gaddafi. The media world has grown so much. It needs to be fed, fed, fed, with an almost obnoxious demand for more tragedy, more celebrity, more horror.

Olivia Williams, www.huffingtonpost.co.uk, 31 October 2011